11/05

Japanese Cooking

THE HEALTHY AND NATURAL WAY

First published in 1991 by
Sally Milner Publishing Pty Ltd
17 Wharf Road
Birchgrove NSW 2041 Australia

© Koji Nakano & Lesley Howard Murdoch, 1991

Production by Sylvana Scannapiego,
Island Graphics
Design and illustrations by Doric Order
Typeset in Australia by Asset Typesetting Pty Ltd
Printed in Australia by Australian Print Group

National Library of Australia
Cataloguing-in-Publication data:

Murdoch, Lesley Howard
    Japanese cooking.

    Includes index.
    ISBN 1 86351 021 4.

    1. Cookery, Japanese. I. Nakano, Koji. II. Title.
    (Series: Milner healthy living cookbook)

641.5952

Distributed in Australia and New Zealand by
Transworld Publishers

Japanese Cooking

THE HEALTHY AND NATURAL WAY

Koji Nakano and Lesley Howard Murdoch

SALLY MILNER PUBLISHING

CONTENTS

健康食品

Healthy and Natural Japanese Foods

Healthy Japanese Foods

*M*any best selling cookbooks of the eighties and nineties reflect the principals of Nathan Pritikin's dietary advice in preventing coronary/cancer diseases and contributing to a more healthy way of living. Natural products such as fish, vegetables and grains are recommended, with the intake of animal proteins being reduced as well as that of fats, salt and sugar.

Healthy approaches to diet are not just a recent phenomenon! The Japanese have always been aware of the importance of fresh and natural foods. They eat more fish than any other country, most of it usually raw, seaweed and fresh vegetables. They also have one of the lowest rates of heart disease and live longer than their western counterparts.

The secrets of Japanese cuisine have been introduced to Australians through Japanese restaurants, giving diners an opportunity to sample such delights as **sushi** and **sashimi**, **yakitori**, **tonkatsu** and **tempura**. This combined with the opening up of many Tokyo marts and health food shops selling essential ingredients such as **dashi** and **nori** means that Japanese dishes can now be easily prepared at home.

This carefully selected collection of appetising and

practical recipes is a cookbook to be used as well as admired. It illustrates the simple, quick cooking techniques practised by Japanese chefs for centuries and features the use of fresh unprocessed ingredients, so essential for maximising nutritional food value.

A Low-fat/High Fibre Diet

*T*he Japanese eat mainly fish, rice, noodles, *tofu* and vegetables. Dairy products, bread and processed foods are not part of their traditional diet. Japan produces 15 million tonnes of vegetables annually and its per capita consumption of 1200 kilos a year is well above the western average. Americans for instance consume approximately 800 kilos a year of vegetables.

Japanese natural foods have the following characteristics for a healthy diet.

- high in complex carbohydrates and fibre (especially vegetables, grains and legumes)
- low in fat and cholesterol (no dairy products)
- low in meat protein, but high in vegetable protein, soya beans and soy products
- natural rather than processed foods
- low calorie foods (especially fish, rice and *tofu*)

These traditional Japanese types of foods are strongly recommended in the low-fat/high fibre guidelines issued by the Australian Nutrition Foundation. Western diets that are based on processed foods high in fat and low in fibre are considered to be the main dietary cause of coronaries and cancer problems.

So, if you are concerned about your health and diet, Japanese cuisine is well worth considering.

The Japanese Meal

*J*apanese meals always consist of green tea, rice, soup and pickles as the basic dishes. For ordinary meals such as breakfast this is the complete menu. On more formal occasions or when entertaining, a variety of many different small dishes are added. Sweets are usually not served and the meal finishes with tea, rice, soup and pickles. Recipes are based on fresh, natural ingredients both of the area and of the season. The Japanese aim also to preserve the fresh taste of basic ingredients by using natural flavouring agents derived from the land and the sea. The basis of most Japanese dishes is *dashi*, fish stock made from kelp and dried bonito flakes, and soy sauce, made from soya beans.

The Japanese emphasis on natural foods and flavours is so different to the heavily spiced, curried dishes of Asian countries and the rich sauces of French cuisine. Food is kept as close as possible to its natural taste both in preparation and presentation. This reflects the Japanese philosophy of simplicity and harmony. Serving dishes compliment the food.

Food Presentation

*O*n one level is it difficult for non-Japanese to understand the religious and cultural significance of food presentation as an art form, but on a purely aesthetic level the beauty of any dish can be admired and appreciated. Some of the 'rules' of presentation in Japanese cuisine focus on the contrast of opposites where visual appeal is just as important as taste. The asymmetrical number, five, influences much in Japanese cuisine and culture. Cups and glasses come in sets of five. There are five ways of organising food on plates - *yamamori* is a mountain shape, *suigimono* is a slanting pattern like the cedar tree, *hiramori* is used for flat foods, *ayamori* for woven shapes and *yosemori* for group patterns.

Contrasts in colours and shapes are also considered. *Sushi* contrasts white rice with pink tuna. Green *wasabi* garnishes represent a contrast in both colour and shape, as does the curved twist of lemon served with brown *miso* soup. Foods that are round are served on straight dishes.

Food arrangements represent a painting or a landscape, and bowls and dishes reflect the changing seasons. In summer time the emphasis is on creating an atmosphere of coolness. One way of achieving this is to dip unglazed dishes in water which gives the effect of cool water-washed stones. Containers without lids, bamboo utensils, green leaf displays and dishes with patterns of waves or fish swimming all enhance the atmosphere of coolness. Japanese foods served cold include *tofu* and *somen*. Garnishes such as grated ginger and chopped leeks are used to accentuate cool tastes.

Formal Dining

When the Japanese present a formal dinner there is always a set order in the way the dishes are served. Here is an example of a formal menu.

1. Appetiser
2. Clear soup
3. **Sashimi** (raw fish)
4. Grilled fish
5. Steamed dish
6. Simmered dish
7. Deep fried dish
8. Vinegared salad
9. Rice/**miso** soup/pickles
10. Green tea

Note: In winter one-pot dishes, **nabemono**, replace the middle order dishes.

Japanese servings are small by western standards and a variety of dishes are served. Menus vary according to the time of year with fresh foods in season being featured. There are many Japanese soups, salads and main dishes that can be used instead of one main western-type meal. Different cooking techniques are features in preparing foods and soups, which are often served last instead of sweets.

To plan a Japanese dinner party here are some suggested menus, in order of difficulty, using recipes that are in the book.

Beginners

1. *Soup*   Potato and Celery **Miso** Soup
2. **Sashimi**   **Hamachi - Hirazukuri**
3. **Suno-Mono**   Seafood Salad
4. **Sukiyaki**   Beef with Vegetables
5. *Tea*

Average

1. *Soup*   **Asari** Soup
2. **Yakitori**   Skewered Chicken

4

3. **Agedashi-Dofu** — Deep Fried Bean Curd
4. **Nimono** — **Daikon Miso Ni** (White Radish and Pork cooked in **Miso** Paste)
5. **Kayaku-Gohan** — Mixed Rice
6. **Oshinko** — Pickles
7. *Tea*

Advanced

1. *Soup* — **Ushio** Soup
2. **Sashimi** — **Tai-shimofuri-zukuri**
3. **Agemono** — **Gyu-maki-Age**
4. **Mushimono** — **Tori sakamushi** (Steamed Chicken)
5. **Yakimono** — **Nasu-chigiyaki** (Grilled Eggplant with **Miso** Paste)
6. **Nimono** — **Niku-jaga** (Beef and Potato Cooked in Soy Sauce)
7. **Gohan-mono** — **Tori-Zosui** (Chicken Porridge)
8. **Oshinko** — Pickles
9. *Tea*

Japanese Meal Etiquette

*C*ertain customs, courtesies and procedures are followed when the Japanese entertain and where appropriate should be followed when eating in a Japanese restaurant.

- The Japanese table is low, like a coffee table. Guests kneel or sit on cushions, removing their shoes beforehand.
- The hostess is seated at one end near the door, the most important guest is seated opposite her.
- Each guest is presented with a hand-towel to wipe hands and face.
- Food is served individually in small bowls, except for communal one-pot dishes, and eaten with chopsticks.

- Always return chopsticks to their place on the table. Don't cross them, leave them in the food dish or pierce food with them.
- Soup is drunk from the bowl although chopsticks can be used to eat small pieces of meat or vegetable.
- Rice is eaten with chopsticks; the bowl is held in the left hand. *Sushi* may be eaten with fingers.
- Pieces of fruit are not eaten with the fingers.
- *Sake* is shared. Never pour your own glass, pour your neighbours.
- Green tea is served at the table from a pot which is replaced regularly with a fresh one. Japanese tea is different from Chinese tea and is usually drunk at the end of the meal, not with it.
- Tea, wine or *sake* are normally taken independently, not alternatively as many Australians practise.

Buying Japanese Ingredients

*F*ollow the Japanese rule for buying what is in season, especially fresh vegetables, and plan recipes around these. Practise oriental techniques that utilise fresh and natural ingredients. Consider other sources of protein such as soya beans and cook mainly vegetarian dishes with a small amount of protein, preferably fish, chicken or *tofu*. Your food bill will be reduced and your family will be much healthier. Consider also the nutritional value of raw food. Not all vegetables need to be cooked. Many Japanese recipes feature raw or lightly cooked ingredients.

White rice or brown, if you prefer, and noodles are the basic ingredients. For seasonings and stocks you need soy sauce, *miso* paste, *dashi* fish stock and seaweeds. These and other specialist foods such as Japanese pickles, *wasabi* horseradish, *konnyaku* and *mirin* can also be purchased from oriental grocers. *Tofu* purchased fresh or in long life packets or dried is available from most health food shops. A list of Japanese retail outlets follows at the end of this section.

The Ingredients

*T*he Japanese use normal dark soy sauce unless light is specified. In either case a salt-reduced sauce could be substituted, see Glossary.

- *Miso* is also light or dark and either can be used according to taste, unless specified.
- Different seaweeds are used for different purposes, e.g. *nori* for *sushi* and garnishes, *wakame* for other dishes and *konbu* mostly for *dashi* stock/soups, and must be specified.
- Bean curd is the English word for *tofu*. *Tofu* comes in blocks or cakes about the same size, but is variable, e.g. fresh or long life comes in 297g, (10½oz) packets, which would serve 4 soups. A piece of *aburage* is 5x10cm — similar to a slice of cheese, or a *nori* sheet.
- Ingredients such as *miso* noodles generally come in packages of 200 or 250g; *Konnyaku* again comes in a block of 200g.
- The Japanese do use small amounts of sugar and salt in their recipes. These could be omitted, if desired, in most cases.
  Note: The overall aim has been to try and simplify these recipes for Australian cooks who are trying to learn Japanese cooking.

Japanese Foods Retail Shops in Australia

NSW

Super Sakura — 02 958 7947
9/100 Edinbough Road,
Castlecrag, NSW 2068

Tokyo Mart — 02 958 6860
Shop 27, Northbridge Plaza,
Northbridge, NSW 2063

Anegawa Trading — 02 406 5452
16A Deepwater Road,
Castlecove, NSW 2069

Ichibankan — 02 247 2667
36 Nurses Walk,
The Rocks, NSW 2000

Katsurack — 02 953 1183
Shop 8, The Grove, 166-174 Military Road,
Neutral Bay, NSW 2089

Burlington Centre — 02 281 2777
TG9 Prince Centre, Thomas Street,   211 2353
Ultimo, NSW 2000

David Jones Market St Store — 02 266 5544
86-108 Castlereagh Street,
Sydney, NSW 2000

VIC

Suzuran Japanese Foods — 03 882 2349
1025 Burke Road,
Hawthorn VIC 3122

Japan Mart — 03 51 9882
568 Malvern Road,   51 9344
Prahran, VIC 3181

Tokyo Mart — 03 523 6200
584 Glenhuntly Road,
Elsternwick, VIC 3187

Miyajima Food Centre — 03 570 3321
2 Sanicki Court,
East Bentleigh, VIC 3165

WA

Benjamin & Co Pty Ltd ⸺ 09 328 6326
88 Beaufort Street,   328 6341
Perth, WA 6000

Nippon Food Distributor ⸺ 09 388 2738
479 Hay Street,
Subiaco, WA 6008

Nishida Japanese Food Centre ⸺ 09 325 3929
113 Murny Street,
Perth, WA 6000

QLD

B.G. Supermarket ⸺ 07 252 2242
Cnr Ann Street & Marchal Distributors,   252 2246
Fortitude, QLD 4006

Japan Mart ⸺ 07 371 5891
Shop 2, 191 Moggill Road,
Taringa, QLD 4068

Oriental Produce Trading ⸺ 075 96 3633
Shop 4, Damar Ctr. Lavelle Street,
Nerang, QLD 4211

Chinatown Cookshop ⸺ 070 51 1199
West Court Plaza, Mulgrave Road,
Cairns, QLD 4870

SA

Kouche Oriental Supermarket ⸺ 08 212 7130
88 Gouger Street,
Adelaide, SA 5000

汁物

Stocks and Soups

Stocks and Soups

*S*oup is an essential part of every Japanese meal. In western cuisine, soup is usually the first course at an evening meal, but in Japan it is served for breakfast or with rice and pickles as a final course for a formal dinner. **Suimono,** a clear soup, is taken between courses to refresh the palate, similar to the way in which the French use sorbets.

Soup is served piping hot in lacquered bowls that conserve the heat. Soups are presented artistically with contrasting coloured garnishes to complete a landscape pattern. To eat soup remove the solid ingredients with chopsticks and sip the liquid by holding the bowl up to your mouth.

The 'secret' or unique ingredient to Japanese cuisine is a 'good' **dashi**. This is the mark of excellence for a chef. As well as a soup base it is the simmering stock for many cooked dishes. For convenience it is recommended to use instant fish stock **dashi** available from oriental grocers, or you can make your own using this recipe.

だし
DASHI
Fish Stock

This is the basic stock for almost all Japanese soups and can be purchased as an instant packet mix (similar to beef or chicken stock cubes) available in Asian grocery shops, or you can make your own using this recipe.

15cm square **konbu**
  dried seaweed
10g bonito dried
  mackerel flakes
4 cups of water

1. Soak seaweed in water until soft. When softened put saucepan over heat and almost bring water to the boil.
2. Just before water boils, remove seaweed and add fish flakes.
3. Simmer for 10 minutes, then strain to remove the fish flakes.

Stock is now ready to use as base for other soups.

Serves Four

みそ汁
MISO-SHIRU
Miso Soup

> *200g* **daikon** *white
>   radish*
> *1 piece deep-fried* **tofu**
> *2 tablespoons* **miso** *paste*
> *4 cups* **dashi** *stock*

1. Slice **daikon** and **tofu** into 4cm pieces.
2. Pour hot water on **tofu** pieces to remove oil.
3. Boil **daikon** in 2 cups water until soft.
4. Strain the boiling water, add 3 cups of fish stock and mix in white radish and **tofu**.
5. Place **miso** paste in separate pan, stir over low heat until it melts, then add to other ingredients.
6. Bring soup to the boil then turn off immediately.

> *Serves Four*

VARIATIONS

Base

> *2 tablespoons* **miso** *paste*
> *4 cups fish stock* **dashi**

Bean Shoots and Tofu

> *200g bean shoots*
> *1 piece deep-fried* **tofu**

Tofu and Spring Onion

> 120g **tofu** cut into 1cm
> squares
>
> 8 spring onions, sliced

Tofu and Wakame

> 120g **tofu**
>
> 5g **wakame** (soaked in
> water beforehand to
> make 20g)

Tofu and Garlic Chives

> 200g **tofu**
>
> 40g garlic chives,
> chopped

Lettuce and Deep-Fried Tofu

> 100g lettuce, finely sliced
>
> 1 piece deep-fried **tofu**

Potato and Celery

> 120g shredded potato
>
> 40g celery, cut into small
> pieces

白身魚のお吸い物
SHIROMI ZAKANA NO OSUIMONO
White Fish, Spinach and Fish Cake Soup

>*4 x 30g pieces white fish,*
>   *cooked in boiling*
>   *water for 2 minutes*
>*40g spinach, cooked*
>*4 pieces frozen fish cake,*
>   *cooked 1 minute in*
>   *boiling water*
>*4 cups **dashi** stock*

1. Place all ingredients in saucepan, heat through but do not boil.

>*Serves Four*

豆腐と椎茸のお吸物
TOFU-TO-SHIITAKE NO OSUIMONO
Tofu, Spring Onions and Mushroom Soup

> *4 x 5cm square pieces*
> *deep-fried* **tofu**
> *8 spring onions*
> *4* **shiitake** *mushrooms*
> *4 cups* **dashi** *stock*

1. Rinse **tofu** in boiling water and cut into 1cm slices.
2. Cut spring onion into 4cm slices then boil in water for 1 minute.
3. Soak in cold water for 20 minutes and then cook in boiling water for 2 minutes.
4. Combine all ingredients with **dashi** stock and heat.

> *Serves Four*

かきたま汁
KAKITAMA SOUP
Scrambled Egg Soup

> *100g chicken breast*
> *8 spring onions*
> *4 cups **dashi** stock*
> *1 egg, beaten*

1. Boil chicken breast for 5 minutes then cut into small pieces.
2. Chop spring onions into small pieces.
3. Combine chicken and spring onion with **dashi** stock, bring to boil.
4. Stir egg into boiling soup, and serve immediately.

Serves Four

潮汁
USHIO SOUP
(Favourite in Japan)

> 200g snapper including
>   head and bones
> 2 teaspoons salt
> 15cm square **wakame**
>   seaweed
> 5 cups water
> light soy sauce to taste
> 8 spring onions, cut into
>   4cm slices
> 10g shredded ginger
> 2 tablespoons **sake**

1. Cut snapper into small pieces then sprinkle with salt. Allow to stand for 30 minutes. Place in boiling water for 2 minutes then in cold water for 5 minutes. Remove blood and scales.
2. Place **wakame**, snapper and water in large saucepan.
3. Just before water boils remove **wakame**, reduce heat and cook for 12 minutes.
4. Add spring onions, shredded ginger, light soy sauce and **sake**.

> *Serves Four*

あさりのみそ汁
ASARI SOUP
Clam Soup

Can be made with either **miso** paste or fish soup stock **dashi**.

400g clams, scrubbed
4 cups water
2 tablespoons red **miso**
   paste
1 tablespoon light soy
   sauce
2 tablespoons **sake**

1. Soak clams overnight in salty water.
2. Place clams and water in saucepan and boil until shells open.
3. Add the **miso** paste, soy sauce and **sake.**

Serves Four

飯物
うどん、そば

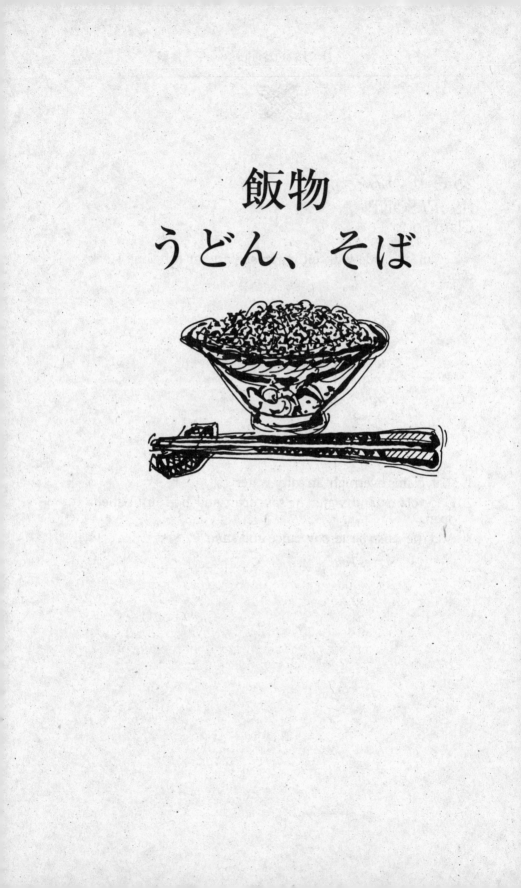

Rice

Rice

Rice *gohan* is the Japanese staple food. It is served at every meal and can be a complete meal itself. Rice with *miso* soup is a common breakfast, served in a bowl *donburi* with a sauce it is a popular luncheon dish, and fluffy white rice is served as a last course at a formal dinner.

The Japanese prefer short grain white rice grown locally. However, the slightly more nutritious brown rice can be substituted in most recipes, increasing the cooking times.

Cooking rice is a difficult skill to master. In Japanese restaurants master chefs may just specialise in cooking perfect rice. Most Japanese families now use an automatic electric rice cooker.

Basic Steamed Rice

Preparation

1. Wash 1 cup white rice in cold water.
2. Remove any refuse.
3. Strain water away.
4. Wash again, using your hand to make a circle about 50 times quickly.
5. Put in water again and strain.
6. Repeat steps until water is clear.

Note: Washing many times is the Japanese 'secret' for good rice.

Cooking Instructions

1. Place rice in 1¼ cups water.
2. Allow to stand for 30 minutes.
3. Put rice in saucepan.
4. Put in 1¼ cups of water (equal amounts of rice and water).
5. Boil for 2 minutes.
6. Reduce heat for 5 minutes.
7. Reduce to very low for 10 minutes.
8. Increase heat to high for 20 seconds then turn off.
9. Leave in saucepan for 15 minutes.
10. Stir rice from bottom gently with wooden spoon.

Serves Four

Electric Rice Cooker

Most Japanese families use an automatic electric rice cooker for convenience. Same amounts and same preparation but leave to dry for 30 minutes before cooking. Automatic cooking takes 25 minutes. Allow rice to stand for 10 minutes and turn switch on again. Drain off excess water.

鳥ぞうすい
TORI-ZOSUI
Chicken Porridge

2½ *cups steamed rice*
200g *chicken breast*
50g *bamboo shoots*
1 *Japanese* **shiitake**
   mushroom
7½ *cups* **dashi** *stock*
2 *tablespoons light soy*
   sauce
2 *teaspoons* **sake**
2 *spring onions, chopped*
2 *eggs, beaten*

1. Place steamed rice in strainer, and rinse under running water.
2. Cut chicken into 2cm squares, and bamboo shoots and Japanese mushroom **shiitake** into 2cm pieces.
3. Boil **dashi** stock and add soy sauce and **sake**.
4. Add rice and boil for 3 minutes.
5. Add chicken, bamboo shoots and mushroom and boil a further 2 minutes.
6. Mix in spring onions and eggs, turn off heat.

   Serves Four

かゆ
KAYU
Simple Porridge

> ½ *cup uncooked white*
> *rice*
> 2½ *cups water*

1. Wash rice and drain.
2. Place rice and water in a saucepan and bring to the boil.
3. Stir gently and boil for 5 minutes.
4. Reduce heat to very low for 25 minutes.

   Serves Four

グリンピースごはん
ENDO-GOHAN
Green Pea Rice

> 2¼ *cups rice*
> ¼ *cup sticky rice*
> 4 *cups water*
> 2 *teaspoons* **mirin**
> ¾ *cup green peas*

1. Rinse rice and sticky rice several times and set aside for 2 hours before cooking.
2. Place rice, water and **mirin** in saucepan.
3. Cook over medium heat until boiling.
4. Add green peas and stir from bottom, then cook for 4 minutes covered.
5. Reduce heat for 8 minutes, increase to high for 20 seconds, then turn off.
6. Leave in saucepan for 10 minutes.
7. Stir and serve.

Serves Four

かやくごはん
KAYAKU-GOHAN
Mixed Rice

20g carrot
60g chicken
1 piece deep-fried **tofu**
2 tablespoons green peas
*3 tablespoons light soy
 sauce*
1 tablespoon **sake**
1 tablespoon **mirin**
3 cups rice
4 cups **dashi** *stock*

1. Cut carrot, chicken and **tofu** into 3cm pieces.
2. Pour boiling water over peas to soften.
3. Mix together soy sauce, **sake** and **mirin** to make sauce.
4. Marinate chicken and **tofu** in sauce for 10 minutes.
5. Rinse rice several times, then drain and set aside for 30 minutes before cooking.
6. Add rice and **dashi** stock to other ingredients (except green peas), and stir until boiling.
7. Reduce heat for 5 minutes then reduce to very low for 15 minutes.
8. Stir in green peas and leave for 10 minutes before serving.

Serves Four

あずきごはん
AZUKI-GOHAN
Red Bean Rice

> *3 cups of rice*
> *¼ cup sticky rice*
> *1²/₃ cups water*
> *½ cup red beans*
> *¾ tablespoon black*
>   *sesame seeds*

1. Rinse rice and sticky rice and drain for 1 hour before cooking.
2. Rinse red beans, place in saucepan with 1²/₃ cups of water and bring to the boil.
3. Discard water then add same amount of cold water.
4. Repeat steps 2 and 3 four times.
5. Drain beans and reserve liquid.
6. Cover beans with cloth.
7. Put rice and the red beans with water to equal 4¼ cups of liquid.
8. Place in saucepan on medium heat and cook as for basic steamed rice.
9. Stir from bottom.
10. Toast black sesame seeds.
11. Place the red bean and rice mixture on plate and sprinkle with sesame seeds.

Serves Four

親子丼
OYAKO-DON
Chicken Rice

4 cups hot steamed rice
150g chicken breast
1 onion
¾ cup **dashi** stock

1 cup **Donburi** *Sauce:*
  ¼ cup soy sauce (low
  salt), ¼ cup **mirin**,
  1 teaspoon sugar,
  1 teaspoon **sake**

4 eggs, beaten
10g **nori** *seaweed*

1. Cut chicken into 2cm pieces.
2. Chop onion into pieces.
3. Put one cup of **dashi** stock with sauce ingredients in a saucepan until boiling to make **Donburi** Sauce.
4. Place **Donburi** Sauce, chicken and onion into saucepan and boil for 2 minutes.
5. Add beaten eggs to mixture and cover with lid for 2 minutes.
6. Serve rice in bowl with other ingredients placed on top.

天丼
TEN-DON
Tempura Rice

> 4 *cups hot steamed rice*
>
> 4 *pieces* **tempura** *prawns*
> (see **Tempura** recipe)
>
> 4 *pieces* **tempura**
> *vegetables (see*
> **Tempura** recipe)
>
> 1 *cup* **Donburi** *Sauce*
> (see **Oyako-Don**)

1. Heat **tempura** pieces.
2. Place rice in bowls with **tempura** on top.
3. Add **Donburi** sauce.

> *Serves Four*

三色丼
SANSHOKU-DONBURI
Three Coloured Rice

4 cups hot steamed rice
200g minced chicken
3 tablespoons soy sauce
    (low salt)
1 tablespoon **mirin**
ground ginger juice to
    taste
3 eggs, beaten
50g green beans

1. Place chicken in saucepan with soy sauce, **mirin** and ginger juice until liquid is absorbed.
2. Scramble eggs in a separate pan.
3. Boil green beans until soft then shred them.
4. Serve rice in bowl with chicken, egg and green beans on top.

   Serves Four

Noodles

Noodles

*N*oodles are Japan's original fast food; cheap, quick, easy to prepare and eaten immediately. Noodles are served with a hot or cold soup and chopsticks are used.

There are two main types of Japanese noodles, those made from buckwheat **soba** and those made from wheat **udon**. **Somen** is a thin wheat noodle served cold in the summer. Vermicelli is a substitute.

Noodle bars are popular in most places, offering handmade noodles **teuchi**. The Japanese eat their noodles with a dipping sauce, usually a mixture of **dashi**, soy and **mirin**.

うどん
UDON
Itsuki-Inaka-Udon

1. Add one packet of **udon** noodles to 4 litres of boiling water.
2. Cook for about 15 minutes, stirring occasionally.
3. Noodles are ready when outside and inside of noodle is the same colour.
4. Allow to stand in saucepan for 10 minutes.
5. Rinse under cold running water and drain.

そば
SOBA
Shin shu-soba

1. Add one packet of **soba** noodles to 4 litres of boiling water.
2. Cook for 5-6 minutes, stirring occasionally.
3. Noodles are ready when soft.
4. Rinse under cold running water and drain.

かけ汁
KAKE GIRU
Basic Hot Noodle Soup

> 4 cups **dashi** stock
> ½ cup soy sauce (low
>   salt)
> 3 tablespoons **mirin**

1. Place ingredients in saucepan and heat until boiling.

> *Serves Four*

天つゆ
TENTSUYU SAUCE
Basic Cold Noodle Soup/Dipping Sauce

> 3 tablespoons **mirin**
> 1½ cups **dashi** stock
> 5 tablespoons soy sauce
>   (low salt)
> 1 tablespoon sugar

1. Place **mirin** in saucepan and bring to the boil.
2. Add all other ingredients and cook for 30 minutes.
3. Allow to cool.

   Serves Four

かけうどん（そば）
UDON OR SOBA
Plain Noodles

1 x 250g packet **udon/**
soba *noodles, cooked*
½ bunch spinach
2 spring onions
chili pepper to taste
4 cups basic hot noodle
soup (see **Kake Giru***)*

1. Place noodles in strainer and pour over boiling water to heat.
2. Divide the noodles among 4 bowls.
3. Boil spinach and chop into 5cm pieces.
4. Chop spring onions into small pieces.
5. Place spinach and spring onion on top of noodles.
6. Add 1 cup of basic hot noodle soup and chili pepper to taste to each bowl.

きつねうどん（そば）
KITSUNE UDON
Noodles with tofu

1 x 250g packet **udon/**
  soba *noodles, cooked*
2 *pieces deep-fried* **tofu**
2 *spring onions, chopped*
1 *cup* **dashi** *stock*
1 *tablespoon* **mirin**
1 *tablespoon sugar*
  (optional)
2 *tablespoons soy sauce*
  (low salt)
4 *cups basic hot noodle*
  soup (see **Kake Giru**)

1. Cut **tofu** into 4 pieces, pour over boiling water to remove oil, drain.
2. Place **tofu** in a saucepan with remaining ingredients (except spring onions).
3. Cook over medium heat until liquid is absorbed.
4. Cut spring onions into 4cm pieces.
5. Reheat noodles in boiling water, drain and place in bowl.
6. Place **tofu** on noodles, divide into 4 serves.
7. Place spring onions on top of each serving.
8. Pour 1 cup of basic hot soup over each serving.

Serves Four

月見うどん
TSUKIMI - UDON
Moon Noodles

> 1 x 250g packet **udon**
>   noodles, cooked
> 2 spring onions, chopped
> 4 eggs
> 1 serve basic hot soup
> chili pepper to taste
> 4 cups basic hot noodle
>   soup (see **Kake Giru**)

1. Place cooked noodles in strainer and pour over boiling water to heat.
2. Divide the noodles among 4 bowls and sprinkle with spring onions.
3. Pour eggs on top to resemble moon.
4. Add basic hot soup, 1 cup per bowl.
5. Serve with chili pepper.

Serves Four

天ぷらうどん（そば）
TEMPURA NOODLES
Prawn Noodles

> *1 x 250g packet* **udon/**
> **soba** *noodles, cooked*
> *8 prawns*
> *½ bunch spinach, cooked*
> *2 spring onions*
>
> *2 cups* **tempura** *batter:*
> *1 cup water, 1 beaten*
> *egg yolk, 1 cup plain*
> *flour mixed together*
>
> *4 cups basic hot noodle*
> *soup (see* **Kake Giru***)*
> *vegetable oil*

1. Shell and devein prawns, leaving tails intact.
2. Heat oil in electric frypan to 170°C, so that batter will rise.
3. Dip prawns in **tempura** batter and deep-fry for 2 minutes.
4. Chop spring onions into small pieces.
5. Reheat noodles by pouring over boiling water, drain then place in bowls.
6. Place **tempura** prawns on top with spinach and spring onions.
7. Add 1 cup of basic hot noodle soup to each bowl.

わかめうどん（そば）
WAKAME UDON
Seaweed Noodles

1 x 250g packet **udon/**
    soba *noodles, cooked*
3 spring onions
1 piece ginger
10g **wakame**
4 pieces fish cake
    kamaboko
4 cups basic hot noodle
    soup (see **Kake Giru***)*

1. Soak **wakame** in cold water for 10 minutes, then cut into 3cm strips.
2. Cut spring onions into 3cm pieces.
3. Peel ginger, shred and place in cold water.
4. Reheat noodles by pouring over boiling water, then place in bowls.
5. Place seaweed, spring onion, fish cake and ginger on top.
6. Add 1 cup basic hot noodle soup to each bowl.

Serves Four

卵とじうどん（そば）
TAMAGO-TOJI-UDON
Egg Noodles

> *1 x 250g packet* **udon/**
> **soba** *noodles, cooked*
> *2 spring onions*
> *4 eggs*
> *2 sheets dried seaweed*
> **nori**
> *4 cups basic hot noodle*
> *soup (see* **Kake Giru***)*

1. Chop spring onions into small pieces.
2. Beat eggs and add to boiling basic hot soup.
3. Reheat noodles by pouring over boiling water, then place in bowls.
4. Remove egg and place with *nori* on top of noodles.
5. Add 1 cup of basic hot soup to each bowl.

   Serves Four

鳥南蛮
TORI-NANBAN
Chicken Noodles

> 1 x 250g packet **udon/**
> **soba** *noodles, cooked*
> *200g chicken pieces*
> *½ bunch spinach*
> *2 spring onions, finely*
> *chopped*
> *4 cups basic hot noodle*
> *soup (see **Kake Giru**)*

1. Cut chicken into 3cm pieces.
2. Boil spinach, drain then cut into 5cm pieces.
3. Add chicken and spring onion to basic soup and cook for 5 minutes.
4. Reheat noodles by pouring over boiling water, then place in bowls.
5. Pour soup with chicken and spring onion over noodles.
6. Add a portion of spinach to each bowl.

Serves Four

肉うどん（そば）
NIKU-UDON
Beef Noodles

1 x 250g packet **udon/**
soba *noodles, cooked*

400g steak, sliced

Cooking Sauce:
  ½ cup **dashi,**
  3 tablespoons soy
  sauce (low salt),
  2 tablespoons **mirin**

2 spring onions, chopped

sesame seeds to taste

4 cups basic hot noodle
  soup (see **Kake Giru**)

1. Cook sliced beef in saucepan with cooking sauce.
2. Reheat noodles by pouring over boiling water, then place in bowls.
3. Add spring onions, beef mixture and sesame seeds.
4. Add 2 cups basic hot noodle soup to each bowl.

   Serves Four

Plate 1: Preparing Sushi Rice

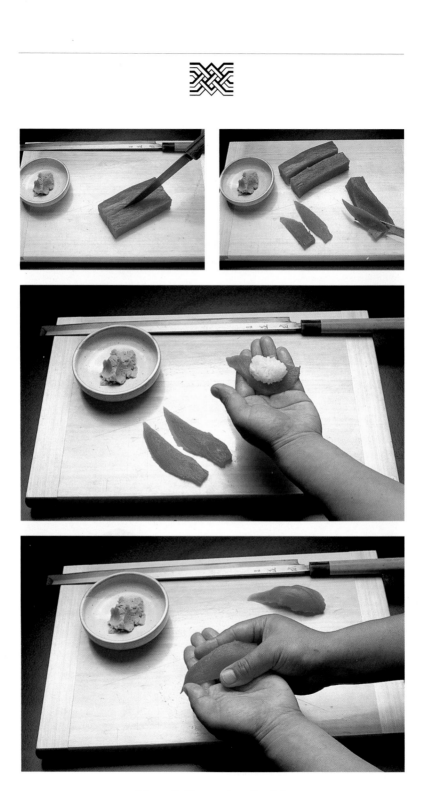

Plate 2: Preparing Sushi

Plate 3: Preparing Rolled Sushi

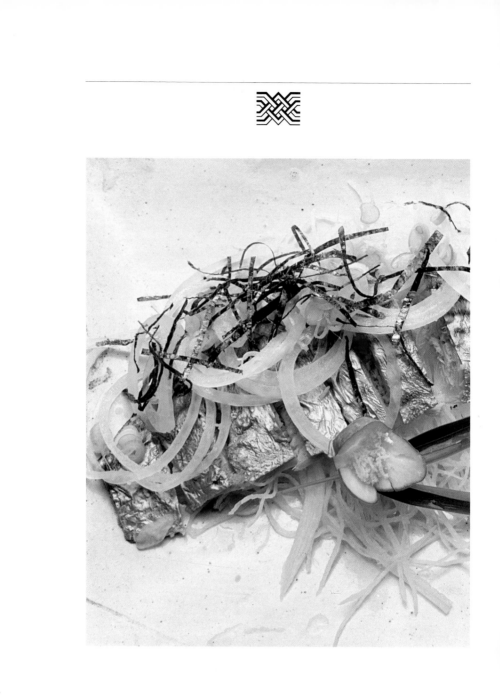

Plate 4: Bonito, grilled and presented Japanese-style

山菜そば
SANSAI SOBA
Vegetable Noodles

> 1 x 250g packet **soba**
>   noodles, cooked
> 1 packet **sansai**
> 2 spring onions, chopped
> 4 cups basic hot noodle
>   soup (see **Kake Giru**)
> hot ground red chili
>   pepper **togarishi-ko**

1. Reheat noodles by pouring over boiling water, then place in bowls.
2. Place **sansai** and spring onions on top of noodles.
3. Add 1 cup basic hot soup to each bowl.
4. Add chili pepper

Serves Four

そうめん
SOMEN
Iced Noodles

4 *bundles* **somen**
  noodles
4 *litres of water*
4 *cups basic cold noodle
  soup (see* **Kake Giru***)*
1 *spring onion, chopped*
1 *ginger, ground*
*ground sesame seeds to
  taste*
wasabi *to taste*

1. Add noodles to 4 litres of boiling water, stir with chopsticks to separate.
2. Simmer for 2 minutes then add ½ cup of cold water, bring to the boil again.
3. Remove noodles immediately, rinse under cold running water then drain and place in bowls with iced water.
4. Serve with basic cold noodle soup and remaining ingredients.
5. In summer add melon/orange/tomato/cherry to the iced water.

Serves Four

みそ煮込みうどん
MISO-NIKOMI UDON
Miso Noodles

200g sliced pork
2 Chinese cabbage leaves
80g red **miso** paste
4 cups **dashi** stock
1 x 250g packet **udon**
   noodles, cooked
½ carrot, chopped
3cm **daikon**, chopped
1 spring onion, chopped

1. Cut pork into 2cm pieces.
2. Cut Chinese cabbage into 3cm pieces.
3. Add red **miso** paste to hot **dashi** stock and stir until melted.
4. Add noodles, pork and other vegetables (except spring onion).
5. Cook for 5 minutes then add spring onion, cook a further 2 minutes.
6. Serve in separate bowls with lids.

Serves Four

寿司とさしみ

Sashimi and Sushi

Sashimi

Sashimi or raw fish is known as Japan's national dish. Its origins can be traced back to 720 AD when Japan's head chef Mut Sukari No Mikoto prepared fresh clams for the emperor.

Though **sashimi** may be described as a simple dish of raw fish it requires a great deal of skill and expertise to prepare and present different types of fish. There are at least ten different ways to cut fish, determined by its size and texture, with many different sharp knives to use.

Sashimi is the most natural and healthiest way to eat fish. It must be absolutely fresh; no frozen fish should be used. Great care and artistry is taken to present the **sashimi**; each platter can be compared to a painting or a landscape.

Soy sauce, freshly grated ginger and horseradish also are served with **sashimi**. It can be eaten as finger food or with chopsticks. Many westerners are wary about tasting raw fish for the first time, but are usually pleasantly surprised by its delicate taste.

Raw fish is a feature of Japanese cuisines but other countries also enjoy it raw. Greeks eat squid and shellfish raw, Swiss eat herrings, and oysters and mussels are usually served natural. The only fish that is not recommended is the poisonous **fugu**; leave that to the Japanese experts.

はまち平造り
HAMACHI-HIRAZUKURI SASHIMI
Kingfish

300g kingfish fillets
*5cm **daikon** white*
*   radish, shredded*
soy sauce (low salt)
*10g **wasabi***

1. Place kingfish on cutting board and cut into 1cm pieces.
2. Arrange **daikon** on plate and place kingfish slices on top.
3. Serve with soy sauce and **wasabi**
    Serves Four

しめさばの八重造り
SHIMESABA-YAE-ZUKURI
Mackerel

300g mackerel fillets
*5cm **daikon**, shredded*
soy sauce (low salt), to
    taste
*10g **wasabi***

Marinade:
    2 cups vinegar and
    50g salt (optional)

1. Sprinkle fish with salt, set aside for 1 hour then wash and pat dry.
2. Marinade fish in vinegar for 30 minutes, remove and pat dry.
3. Remove bones and skin.
4. Cut into 5mm slices.
5. Arrange **daikon** on plate and place mackerel slices on top.
6. Serve with soy sauce and **wasabi**.

   Serves Four

鯛の霜降り造り
TAI-SHIMOFURI-ZUKURI
Snapper

> *300g snapper fillets, with skin*
> *5cm **daikon** white radish, finely shredded*
> *soy sauce (low salt)*
> *10g **wasabi***

1. Pour boiling water on skin side of snapper, plunge immediately into iced water then pat dry.
2. Cut snapper into 1.5cm squares.
3. Arrange snapper on shredded **daikon**.
4. Serve with soy sauce and **wasabi.**

   Serves Four

かつお、たたき造り
KATSUO-TATAKI
Bonito

*300g bonito fillets, with
    skin*
2 spring onions, chopped
30g ground ginger
1 clove garlic

*Special Sauce:
    1 tablespoon vinegar,
    1 tablespoon soy sauce
    (low salt), 1 teaspoon
    sugar*

1. Arrange bonito fillets on skewers and sear skin over high heat.
2. Plunge immediately in iced water, remove skewers and pat dry.
3. Cut bonito into 1cm squares, add remaining ingredients including Special Sauce and heat lightly.
4. Refrigerate for 1 hour then serve.

Serves Four

まぐろの霜降り造り
MAGURO-SHIMOFURI-ZUKURI
Tuna

300g tuna fillets
*5cm **daikon** white
    radish, shredded*
soy sauce (low salt)
*10g **wasabi***

1. Cut tuna into 2cm squares, place in boiling water then plunge immediately into iced water and pat dry.
2. Cut tuna into 1cm pieces.
3. Place tuna on top of shredded **daikon**.
4. Serve with soy sauce and **wasabi**.

Serves Four

Sushi

Sushi is a delightful combination of vinegared rice with raw fish and or pickles, eggs, cucumber or omelette. It is eaten with fingers or chopsticks and served with ginger and soy sauce.

Sushi originated as a way of preserving fish. Today it is made with only the freshest fish and in *sushi* bars the special rice is often made three times a day.

Creating perfect *sushi* is an exacting art. Japanese *sushi* chefs serve a ten year apprenticeship beginning with learning how to make vinegared rice, selecting and slicing the varieties of fish and finally the artistic presentation of *sushi* with complimentary patterns, textures, colours, tastes and garnishes.

There are many different types of *sushi*. The most common is rolled *sushi nori-maki*. This is made by placing a sheet of toasted *nori* seaweed on a bamboo rolling mat, covering it with vinegared rice, adding the appropriate fillings and rolling it up.

Sushi may be the most difficult Japanese cuisine to master, however rolled combinations using a variety of fillings make an ideal picnic or office lunch or a stunning entree for a dinner party.

寿司ご飯
SUSHI GOHAN
Sushi Rice

> *4 cups uncooked rice*
> *½ cup rice vinegar*
> *1 tablespoon sugar*
> *1 tablespoon salt*
> *(optional)*

1. Wash rice and set aside 2 hours before using.
2. Place rice in saucepan with 4½ cups of water.
3. Allow to boil for 5 minutes, reduce heat for 20 minutes then turn off.
4. Allow rice to stand for 15 minutes.
5. Mix together vinegar, sugar and salt, if using.
6. Place the rice in a wide bowl and add vinegar mix.
7. Using a rice spoon lightly mix the rice and vinegar mix.
8. Fan rice by hand until cool.

Serves Four

巻き寿司
NORI-MAKI SUSHI
Rolled Sushi

4 sheets **nori**
900g **sushi** *rice*
40g tuna fillets
wasabi *to taste*

(bamboo mat for rolling)

1. Place 1 sheet of **nori** on bamboo mat.
2. Spread a quarter of the rice over **nori**, leaving 1cm edges.
3. Spread tuna and **wasabi** in a line along the middle.
4. Roll up from bottom to top.
5. Cut into 6 or 8 pieces.

   Serves Four

にぎり寿司
NIGIRI SUSHI
Rice and Raw Fish

> *600g* **sushi** *rice*
>
> *assorted fish fillets*
>   *(tuna/kingfish/*
>   *snapper/smoked*
>   *salmon/cooked*
>   *prawn/garfish/*
>   *cuttlefish)*
>
> **wasabi**

1. Cut fillets into 3 x 6cm pieces.
2. Pick up one piece of fish with left hand, place a little **wasabi** on one side and then top with rice.
3. Turn over rice and fish and using 2 fingers (index and middle finger) press together.
4. Turn clockwise and press again.

> *1 serve is 8 small pieces of fish*

ふくさ寿司
FUKUSASUSHI
Egg Sushi

*300g **sushi** rice*

Sushi *omelette:*
  12 eggs, 3 tablespoons
  sugar, 1 teaspoon
  cornflour, 1 teaspoon
  water

8 prawns, cooked

*8 **shiitake** mushrooms*

1 piece ginger

Special Sauce:
  *½ cup **dashi** stock,*
  1½ tablespoons sugar,
  1½ tablespoons
  ***mirin**, 1 tablespoon*
  soy sauce (low salt),
  vegetable oil

1. Beat together omelette ingredients.
2. Heat oil in pan, divide omelette mixture into 8 and cook one at a time.
3. Peel prawns.
4. Soak **shiitake** for 20 minutes in cold water and cook in Special Sauce.
5. Peel ginger, shred and rinse in cold water.
6. Mix **sushi** rice with **shiitake**, ginger and vinegar.
7. Divide **sushi** rice into 8 portions.
8. Place one portion of rice and one prawn in middle of each omelette and wrap.

いなり寿司
INARI-ZUSHI
Deep-fried Tofu Sushi

320g **sushi** rice
8 pieces deep-fried **tofu**

Special Sauce No. 1:
   ½ cup **dashi** stock,
   2 tablespoons soy
   sauce (low salt),
   2 tablespoons **mirin**,
   2 tablespoons **sake**,
   2 tablespoons sugar

Special Sauce No. 2:
   ½ cup **dashi** stock,
   1½ tablespoons sugar,
   1½ tablespoons **mirin**,
   1 tablespoon soy sauce
   (low salt)

1 piece ginger
4 **shiitake** mushrooms
2 tablespoons sesame
   seeds

1. Pour hot water over deep-fried **tofu** to remove oil, drain.
2. Place **tofu** and Special Sauce No. 1 in saucepan and cook until absorbed.
3. Peel ginger, shred and rinse in cold water.
4. Soak **shiitake** in cold water, cut into small pieces, then cook in Special Sauce No. 2.
5. Heat **sushi** rice and **sushi** vinegar then let cool.
6. Add ginger, sesame seeds and mushrooms.
7. Divide **sushi** rice into 8 portions and place a piece of **tofu** inside each portion.

Serves Four

五目ちらし
GOMOKU-CHIRASHI
Mixed Vegetable Sushi

4 *cups* **sushi** *rice*

1 *piece ginger*

100g *carrots*

10g **shiitake** *mushrooms*

50g *boiled bamboo
    shoots*

50g *green beans*

2 *pieces* **sushi** *omelette
    (see* **Fukusasushi***)*

5 *tablespoons sesame
    seeds*

1 *sheet* **nori** *seaweed*

Special Sauce:

1 *cup* **dashi** *stock,
3 tablespoons sugar,
2 tablespoons* **mirin***,
2 tablespoons* **sake***,
3 tablespoons light soy
sauce, 1 teaspoon salt
(optional)*

1. Prepare **sushi** rice.
2. Peel ginger, shred and rinse in cold water.
3. Peel carrots and cut into 4cm long pieces.
4. Soak **shiitake** in cold water and cut into small pieces.
5. Chop bamboo shoots into small pieces.
6. Shred omelette into small pieces.

7. Boil green beans in salted water, cool and cut into small pieces.

8. Put all vegetables in saucepan and add Special Sauce, cook about 20 minutes on medium heat.

9. Mix vegetables and **sushi** rice.

10. Place mixed **sushi** rice on a plate or in a bowl, and serve with sesame seeds, omelette and seaweed.

Serves Four

肉料理
海鮮料理

Meat and Fish

Cooking Meat and Fish

*T*here are five ways of cooking meat and fish, all of which seek to retain the natural flavour and nutritional value of the ingredients. They are similar to western cooking techniques and include grilling, steaming, simmering and deep-frying as well as one-pot cooking at the table. Most Japanese do not own stoves, so oven cooking is not practised.

Grilling *Yakimono*

Most fish and meat is cooked over a direct flame, using a **hibachi** grill holder. It may be marinated in **sake** or **mirin** before cooking. A gas barbecue or western style oven grill may be used.

Simmering *Nimono*

This is the most common cooking method. The Japanese use a drop lid saucepan **otoshi-buta** which keeps the ingredients submerged in the simmering stock. **Dashi, miso,** soy and **mirin** are the basic stock ingredients.

Steaming *Mushimo*

Steaming is a quick and simple cooking method. Often steaming baskets which sit over a dish of water can be used. Steaming enhances colour and retains the nutritional value of food.

Deep-frying *Agemono*

Deep-frying is often thought of as a fatty way of cooking food but Japanese food is never greasy. Vegetable oil is kept at a very high temperature which seals the outside and allows the inside to cook by radiation. The Japanese use chopsticks but tongs can also be used.

One-pot *Nabemono*

One-pot originated from early times when there was always a soup kettle hanging over the hearth. Combinations of ingredients are prepared and cooked at the table over a gas ring or in an electric frypan. Guests can select pieces to cook and later dip them in selections of sauces before eating.

Meat and Fish Cooking Techniques

Technique	Examples
ONE-POT *Nabemono*	*Sukiyaki*
	Tori Mizutaki
	Oden
	Kaki-Miso-Saki
STEAM *Mushimo*	*Tori-Sakamushi*
	Chilli-Mushi
SIMMER *Nimono*	*Ebi-Shiitake*
	Saba-Misoni
GRILL *Yakimono*	*Shogayaki*
	Yakitori
	Teriyaki
	Tataki
	Kushikatsu
	Ika-Teppo-Yaki
DEEP-FRY *Agemono*	*Tempura*
	Tonkatsu
	Gyu-Maki-Age
	Karei-Kara-Age
	Nanban Zuke

牛肉たたき
BEEF TATAKI
Japanese Rare Beef

300g beef fillet
1 tablespoon vegetable
*   oil*
salt and pepper to taste
ground garlic to taste
ground ginger to taste
3 spring onions, chopped
Japanese orange vinegar

1. Sprinkle salt, pepper and garlic on beef and allow to stand for 1 hour.
2. Heat oil in pan and brown beef on high heat for 2 minutes then reduce heat to low and cook, covered, for 10 minutes.
3. Remove beef from pan and immediately place in iced water, pat dry.
4. Slice beef into small pieces and arrange on plate.
5. Serve with orange vinegar, chopped onions and ginger.

Serves Four

牛肉の巻き揚げ
GYU-MAKI-AGE
Deep-fried Beef

8 pieces beef scotch fillet
salt and pepper to taste
  (optional)
1 carrot
1 celery stick
green beans, cut into
  16 long strips
plain flour
1 egg, beaten
1 cup breadcrumbs
oil for deep-frying

1. Sprinkle salt and pepper on beef (optional).
2. Peel carrot and celery and cut into long strips.
3. Boil carrot, celery and green beans.
4. Roll vegetables inside beef pieces.
5. Roll in flour, dip in beaten egg, then coat with breadcrumbs.
6. Deep-fry at 170°C for approximately 5 minutes until cooked.
7. Cut beef into 3cm pieces and arrange on plate.

   Serves Four

肉じゃが
NIKU-JAGA
Beef and Potato in Soy Sauce

200g sliced beef fillet
600g potatoes
1 small carrot
2 onions
½ cup **somen** noodles
2½ tablespoons oil

Special Sauce:
  6 tablespoons soy
  sauce (low salt),
  2½ tablespoons sugar,
  1 tablespoon **mirin**,
  1 tablespoon **sake**,
  50g canned peas

1. Cut beef into 4cm pieces.
2. Peel potatoes and cut into 4 cm squares.
3. Peel carrot and cut into 5mm pieces.
4. Peel onions and cut each into 8 pieces.
5. Soften **somen** in hot water, drain and cut into 8 pieces.
6. Heat oil in saucepan and brown beef, potato, carrot, onion and **somen**.
7. Add water and Special Sauce to cover and cook for 20 minutes on low heat.
8. Add peas and cook for another 5 minutes.

Serves Four

串カツ
KUSHIKATSU
Skewered Pork

200g shoulder pork
2 onions
salt and pepper
  (optional)
1 egg, beaten
1 cup plain flour
1 cup breadcrumbs
oil for deep-frying
80g cabbage, shredded
English mustard to taste
1 lemon, sliced
1 cup **tonkatsu** *sauce*

1. Cut pork and onion into 2cm pieces.
2. Thread pork and onion onto skewers.
3. Sprinkle with salt and pepper (optional).
4. Roll in flour, dip in beaten egg, then coat with breadcrumbs.
5. Deep-fry skewered pork.
6. Serve on plate with cabbage, mustard, lemon and **tonkatsu** sauce

Serves Four

豚肉しょうが焼
SHOGAYAKI
Ginger Pork

600g shoulder pork,
thinly sliced
100g onion, sliced
100g bean shoots

Shogayaki *Sauce:*
4 tablespoons soy
sauce (low salt),
2 tablespoons **mirin,**
2 tablespoons **sake,**
ginger juice and
ground garlic

sesame seeds to taste
oil for frying

1. Fry pork in pan for 2 minutes then add onion and bean shoots.
2. Add **Shogayaki** Sauce and cook on medium heat until onion is soft.
3. Arrange the pork on plate and sprinkle with sesame seeds.

    Serves Four

大根と豚肉のみそ煮
DAIKON MISO NI
White Radish and Pork in Miso Paste

500g **daikon** *white radish*

300g *shoulder pork*

1 **konnyaku**

10g **nori** *seaweed*

garlic to taste

sliced ginger to taste

1 tablespoon vegetable oil

1 teaspoon instant **dashi** *stock*

2 tablespoons sugar

2 tablespoons **sake**

3 tablespoons **miso** *paste*

3 cups water

1. Peel and slice **daikon**.
2. Cut pork into 2cm pieces.
3. Cut **konnyaku** into 1cm pieces.
4. Soak **nori** in water then cut into 10cm pieces and tie up.
5. Place vegetable oil, garlic, ginger, pork, **daikon** and **konnyaku** in saucepan and brown.
6. Add 3 cups water, instant **dashi**, sugar, **sake**, 2 tablespoons **miso** paste and **nori** and cook, covered for 40 minutes over low heat.
7. When vegetables are soft add 1 tablespoon of **miso** paste.

Serves Four

71

焼鳥
YAKITORI
Skewered Chicken

200g chicken fillets
1 bunch spring onions
chili pepper to taste

Yakitori *Sauce:*
  2 tablespoons soy
  sauce (low salt),
  1 tablespoon sugar,
  1 tablespoon **mirin***,*
  1 tablespoon **sake**

oil

1. Combine **Yakitori** Sauce ingredients and cook for 1 hour over low heat.
2. Cut chicken fillets into 2cm pieces and spring onion (white part only) into 2cm pieces.
3. Thread chicken and onion onto skewers.
4. Fry skewered chicken over medium heat.
5. Pour **Yakitori** Sauce over chicken just before serving.
6. Arrange chicken on plate and sprinkle with chili pepper
   Serves Four

照り焼チキン
TORI-TERIYAKI
Teriyaki Chicken

4 chicken thighs
sansho *to taste*

Teriyaki *Sauce:*
   2 tablespoons soy
   sauce (low salt),
   1 tablespoon sugar,
   2 tablespoons **mirin**,
   1 tablespoon **sake**

oil for frying

1. Combine **Teriyaki** Sauce ingredients and cook for 1 hour over low heat.
2. Cut chicken into even sized pieces.
3. Lightly fry the chicken pieces, cover and cook for about 7 minutes.
4. Add **Teriyaki** Sauce on chicken, cook for 1 minute more.
5. Place chicken on plate, serve with **sansho**.

   Serves Four

鶏の水炊き
TORI MIZUTAKI
Chicken with Vegetables

1 x size 15 chicken
¹/₃ **daikon** white radish
1 carrot
¼ Chinese cabbage,
    chopped
4 **shiitake** mushrooms

4 tablespoons ground
    daikon
chili pepper to taste
2 spring onions, chopped
1 lemon, sliced

Ponzu-Soy Sauce:
¼ cup orange vinegar,
¼ cup soy sauce (low
salt), ¼ cup **dashi**

1. De-bone chicken, chop off legs and wings. Cut flesh into small pieces.
2. Peel **daikon** and carrot, cut into 1cm lengths and boil for 10 minutes.
3. Pour hot water over chicken to remove oil.
4. Simmer chicken pieces in water for 30 minutes, occasionally skimming off fat.
5. Add **daikon**, carrots, Chinese cabbage and **shiitake**, cook a further 3 minutes.
6. Mix ground **daikon** and chili pepper.
7. Mix **Ponzu**-Soy Sauce ingredients together.
8. Serve steam boat at table using **Ponzu**-Soy Sauce and chili/**daikon** as dips.

Serves Four

鳥酒蒸し
TORI-SAKAMUSHI
Steamed Chicken

200g chicken fillet
*1 block of **tofu***
5 spring onions

Special Sauce:
  2 cups bonito stock,
  *3 tablespoons **sake**,*
  2 tablespoons light soy
  sauce

ginger juice to taste

1. Prick chicken with fork and cut into 1cm pieces.
2. Place chicken in boiling water for 1½ minutes and pat dry.
3. Cut **tofu** into 2cm pieces.
4. Cut each spring onion into 4 pieces then slice lengthwise.
5. Divide **tofu** and chicken among 4 bowls, add Special Sauce and cover with lid or foil.
6. Steam each bowl for 15 minutes on medium heat.
7. Remove bowls from steamer, serve with spring onion and ginger juice.

   Serves Four

酢の物
SUNO-MONO
Seafood Salad

4 small mackerel
(squid, sardine or octopus
may be substituted)
1 tablespoon salt
(optional)
2 teaspoons white
vinegar
1 cucumber

Salad Dressing:
1½ tablespoons white
vinegar, 1 tablespoon
mirin, *1 tablespoon*
soy sauce (low salt)

1. Fillet the mackerel, removing all bones.
2. Sprinkle salt on fish and allow to stand for 20 minutes.
3. Wash fish and pat dry.
4. Pour white vinegar over fish and allow to stand for 20 minutes, pat dry.
5. Remove skin from fish and chop flesh into small pieces.
6. Slice cucumber into small pieces.
7. Arrange mackerel and cucumber in a salad bowl and pour Salad Dressing over top.

Serves Four

さばの味噌煮
SABA-MISONI
Spanish Mackerel

1 Spanish mackerel

Marinade:
1½ cups water,
5 tablespoons **miso**
paste, 2½ tablespoons
sugar, 2 tablespoons
sake

1 piece ginger, sliced
1 chili pepper, chopped
2 spring onions, chopped

1. Cut Spanish mackerel into 3cm pieces, wash in salted water and pat dry.
2. Place 2/3 of Marinade in a shallow pan with ginger and chili pepper and bring to the boil.
3. Add mackerel and cook for 10 minutes.
4. Add remaining Marinade and cook on high heat for a further 2 minutes.
5. Serve topped with spring onion.

Serves Four

かれいのから揚げ
KAREI-KARA-AGE
Deep-Fried Flounder

2 flounder
½ cup rice flour
oil for deep-frying
1 spring onion, chopped

Special Sauce:
*   3 tablespoons vinegar,*
*   3 tablespoons light*
*   soy sauce*

1. Fillet flounder, divide into 4 pieces.
2. Coat flounder with rice flour.
3. Heat oil and deep-fry flounder until cooked.
4. Place the flounder on a plate and serve with Special Sauce and spring onion.

   Serves Four

ぶりの角煮
BURI-KAKUNI
Kingfish

300g kingfish, filleted
1 tablespoon salt
4 tablespoons **sake**
1 piece ginger, sliced
½ cup soy sauce
  (low salt)
1 tablespoon sugar
2 tablespoons **mirin**

1. Cut kingfish into 2cm squares.
2. Sprinkle with salt and allow to stand for 10 minutes (optional).
3. Pour boiling water over fish.
4. Heat **sake** and sliced ginger in saucepan with 1/3 of the soy sauce.
5. Add fish and cook over medium heat for 20 minutes.
6. Add the sugar and remaining soy sauce and cook for a further 20 minutes.
7. Add **mirin** and cook slowly for 5 minutes.

   Serves Four

いかぬた
IKA-NUTA
Cuttlefish

> *200g cuttlefish, cleaned*
> *1 tablespoon soy sauce*
>   *(low salt)*
> *½ bunch spring onions*
> *5 tablespoons **miso** paste*
> *5 tablespoons **mirin***
> *1 tablespoon sugar*
> *1½ tablespoons English*
>   *mustard*
> *2 tablespoons white*
>   *vinegar*

1. Chop cuttlefish into small pieces and place in bowl with soy sauce.
2. Cook the spring onions in boiling water, cut into 2cm pieces then add to cuttlefish in bowl.
3. Combine **miso** paste, **mirin**, sugar, mustard and vinegar, and heat in saucepan to make a sauce.
4. Allow sauce to cool before pouring over cuttlefish.

   Serves Four

いかの鉄砲焼
IKA-TEPPO-YAKI
Squid

4 tubes squid
1 spring onion, chopped
10g walnuts, chopped

Special Sauce:
    *4 tablespoons **miso***
    paste, 1 tablespoon
    sugar

1. Clean squid and peel off the skin (use a chux cloth to do this.
2. Mix chopped spring onion and walnut with Special Sauce and divide into 4 servings.
3. Stuff squid tubes with this mixture and secure with toothpicks.
4. Grill the squid until cooked, approximately 5-6 minutes.
5. Cut squid into 2cm slices and arrange on dish.

   Serves Four

平あじの煮つけ
HIRA AJI-NITSUKE
Silver Bream

4 silver bream fillets
100g green beans

Special Sauce:
1 piece sliced ginger,
1½ cups water,
5 tablespoons soy
sauce (low salt),
2 tablespoons **sake**,
1 tablespoon **mirin**,
1½ tablespoons sugar

1. Cut fillets in half to make 8 pieces.
2. Boil green beans and cut into 4cm pieces.
3. Place Special Sauce ingredients in shallow pan and heat until mixed.
4. Add the silver bream and cook for 7 minutes over low heat.
5. Turn heat to medium for 7 minutes on low heat.
6. Add green beans and cook for a further 2 minutes.
7. Place silver bream and green beans on plate, pour the hot sauce on top.

Serves Four

白身魚の南蛮漬
NANBAN-ZUKE
Deep-Fried Marinated Fish

2 white fish fillets
1 teaspoon salt
1 teaspoon white pepper
1 spring onion
½ stick celery
30g carrot
1 green pepper

Special Sauce:
    ¹/₃ cup white vinegar,
    1½ tablespoons
    light soy sauce,
    2 tablespoons
    vegetable oil

1 chili pepper
rice flour for coating
oil for deep-frying

1. Cut the fish into 2cm pieces and sprinkle with salt and pepper.
2. Shred vegetables.
3. Mix Special Sauce ingredients and add chili pepper.
4. Coat fish with rice flour and deep-fry until cooked.
5. Place fish in sauce and add shredded vegetables.

Serves Four

ちり蒸し
CHILLI-MUSHI
Steamed Fish

> 1 *piece* **tofu**
> 150g *white fish fillets*
> 4 *prawns*
> 4 **shiitake** *mushrooms*
> 4 x 8cm *square sheets*
>   **nori** *seaweed*
> 8 *teaspoons* **sake**
>
> *Special Sauce:*
>   *5 tablespoons orange*
>   *vinegar, 5 tablespoons*
>   *soy sauce (low salt),*
>   *10 tablespoons* **dashi**
>   *stock*

1. Cut **tofu** into 4cm pieces.
2. Cut fish into 2cm pieces.
3. Shell the prawns.
4. Remove stems from mushrooms.
5. Divide the above ingredients among 4 cooking bowls and add **nori** to each bowl.
6. Add 2 teaspoons of **sake** to each bowl.
7. Steam for 12 minutes on medium heat.
8. Serve with cold Special Sauce.

Serves Four

ぶりの照り焼
SAKANA-TERIYAKI
Teriyaki Fish

4 x 80g trevally fillets

Teriyaki Sauce:
  3 tablespoons soy
  sauce (low salt),
  5 tablespoons **mirin**,
  1 tablespoon sugar

1. Heat **Teriyaki** Sauce in saucepan for 30 minutes.
2. Cook trevally under high grill.
3. Place ¼ of Sauce on fish and turn grill to medium.
4. Baste with remaining Sauce a few times until cooked.

   Serves Four

鯛の塩焼
TAI-NO-SHIOYAKI (Snapper)

黒鯛の塩焼
KURO-DAI-NO-SHIOYAKI (Bream)

平鰺の塩焼
HIRA-AJI-NO-SHIOYAKI (Silver Bream)
Charcoal Grilled Fish

Cooking a whole fish over a charcoal grill is usually reserved for special occasions such as birthdays or weddings. The fish is served on a plate with a simple garnish of lemon slices.

1. Remove scales and clean fish.
2. Sprinkle salt on fins and tail and cover these parts with foil.
3. Grill over charcoal approximately 8 minutes for the first side and 6 minutes for the second side.
4. Serve on an ornamental plate (head to the left, tail to the right) with a garnish of sliced lemon.

かきのみそすき
KAKI MISO SUKI
Oyster Steam Boat

300g shelled oysters
10 spring onions
1 tin golden mushrooms
 nameko
½ packet vermicelli
½ block of **tofu**

Special **Miso** *Paste:*
 90g red **miso** *paste,*
 70g sugar,
 2 tablespoons **sake**,
 dashi *stock in 3 cups*
 of water

10cm square **kobu** (kelp)

1. Wash oysters in running water.
2. Cut spring onion into diagonal pieces.
3. Pour hot water over mushrooms.
4. Soak vermicelli in hot water and cut into 3 pieces.
5. Cut **tofu** into 1cm pieces.
6. Combine Special **Miso** Paste ingredients and cook over medium heat for 10 minutes.
7. Soak seaweed in water for 30 minutes to make **dashi** stock.
8. Place all ingredients in Steam Boat with Special **Miso** Paste and cook for 15 minutes, adding **dashi** stock occasionally.

えびしいたけ
EBI-SHIITAKE
Prawns with Mushrooms

> 12 *large mushrooms*
>   **shiitake**
> 200g *prawn meat*
> 1½ *tablespoons rice flour*
> 1 *egg white*
> *oil for deep-frying*
> *soy sauce (low salt), for*
>   *serving*

1. Remove stems from mushrooms.
2. Beat prawn meat with knife then mix with rice flour and egg white.
3. Stuff **shiitake** with this mixture.
4. Heat oil to 170°C and cook **shiitake** for 3 minutes.
5. Place **shiitake** on plate, serve with soy sauce.

   Serves Four

栗かぼちゃと干しエビの煮物
KABOCHA-NO-NIMONO
Pumpkin and Prawn in Soy Sauce

½ cup dried prawns

500g pumpkin

*1 tablespoon vegetable
    oil*

2 tablespoons **mirin**

2 tablespoons sugar

*3 tablespoons soy sauce
    (low salt)*

1. Soak dried prawns in water for 3 hours, drain and pat dry.
2. Cut pumpkin into 5cm pieces.
3. Heat oil in pan and brown prawn and pumpkin.
4. Add **mirin**, sugar and water to cover and cook, with the lid on, for 10 minutes.
5. Add soy sauce, increase heat and cook until water is absorbed.

Serves Four

サラダ
野菜料理

Vegetables, Salads and Pickles

Vegetables, Salads and Pickles

Japanese cuisine has one of the most comprehensive and artistic vegetarian cooking in the world. Shojin Ryori developed under the Buddhist religious influence. Even today very little meat is eaten, with the basic diet being rice, noodles, vegetables and pickles.

Vegetables are briefly cooked or served raw to retain their flavour and nutritional value. Salad vegetables are often parboiled and served in an oil-free vinegar. **Summono** are served with vinegar and **aemono** have dressings made from **tofu** and **miso**.

Tsukemono pickled vegetables are served with every meal as an aid to digestion. Pickling developed as a way of preserving vegetables to eat during the long cold winters. The simplest are prepared by salting them and placing them in a barrel or jar with an inner lid weighted down by a stone or brick. This forces the water out and makes them crisper than fresh vegetables and often noisy to chew.

Japanese use many vegetables, including seaweeds, mushrooms, and root vegetables. Most of these can be purchased dried or canned in an Asian grocery shop. White radish **daikon** should be bought fresh and local cabbages, spinach, cucumber and lettuce can be used as substitutes for Japanese varieties.

Japanese Vegetables

*T*he following is a brief description of the Japanese vegetables used in this book. Some are native to Japan and are not grown in Australia.

Dried seaweeds, mushrooms etc are available here. Most health food shops supply freshly made *tofu*. More details are available in the Glossary.

Beans (Soy Beans)

Tofu (Bean Curd)

Tofu is made from soy beans which are softened in water, crushed and then boiled. It is an ideal diet food, high in protein, low in kilojoules.

Tofu should be stored in water in the fridge. Water is changed daily to keep the *tofu* fresh. Long life *tofu* in packets is more convenient to use.

Miso (Soy Bean Paste)

Miso is a high-protein flavouring agent used in many popular Japanese dishes. Tastes and colours vary according to the region in which it is produced and to the different types of soy beans used.

Shinshu *Miso* is a good-tasting brand, light in colour, while Haccho *Miso* is darker and stronger. If the colour is not specified in the recipe any *miso* may be used depending on your taste.

Azuki Beans (Red Beans)

These are steamed with rice for special occasions, or boiled with sugar to make red bean paste, the base for most Japanese sweets.

Mushrooms

Shiitake

These Japanese mushrooms are most commonly used for soups and one-pots. Dried *shiitake* are available in Australia.

Nameko

Tiny button mushrooms used mainly for *miso* soup. They are available in cans.

Matsutake

A special thick mushroom whose growing season is restricted to three weeks a year. It is very expensive and sells for the equivalent of $25 a gram. It grows under the red pine tree and has a magnificent taste and smell.

Served steamed, grilled, or in clear soup. A rare Japanese delicacy, rarer still in Australia!

Enokitake

A very thin mushroom sold in cans. It is white in colour, crisp and used in one-pot dishes.

Seaweeds

Dashi (Fish and Seaweed Stock)

Dashi is a basic stock flavoured with **konbu** and bonito flakes **katsua**.

Shimaya-Dashi-Nomoto (instant powdered **dashi**) can be purchased in oriental grocers.

Konbu (Dried Kelp)

Konbu can be stored in a dark, dry container until ready for use.

Dashi made from **konbu** can be kept 2 or 3 days in the fridge and used for **oden** (vegetable one-pot).

Nori (Fine Seaweed)

Nori comes in rolls for making **sushi**.

Wakame (Leaf Seaweed)

Dried **wakame** needs to be soaked before use in **miso** soup or **sonomono** salads.

Agar-Agar

Made from red seaweed it is a gelatinous substance used for setting sweets and sealing in the flavour of fruits.

Root Vegetables

Konnyaku

This is a grey cake-like substance used as a thickening agent. It has no taste of its own but enhances the natural flavour of other ingredients and is low in kilojoules.

Renkon (Lotus Root)

A crunchy vegetable available dried or canned, which can be used in *tempura* or as a garnish. *Gobo*, very expensive, can also be used in the same way.

Daikon (White Radish)

Grated raw, *daikon* is used as a garnish for *sashimi*; cooked, it can be added to soups and simmered dishes.

Wasabi (Green Horseradish)

This is a paste made from the root of the *wasabi* plant. It is now artificially manufactured because of the cost involved in natural production.

焼きなす
YAKI-NASU
Grilled Eggplant

> *4 eggplants*
> *bonito flakes to taste*
> *ground **daikon***
> *ground ginger to taste*
> *soy sauce (low salt)*

1. Grill eggplants until skin is charred.
2. Remove skins immediately.
3. Cut each eggplant into 5 long pieces, remove stalks.
4. Place eggplant, bonito flakes, *daikon* and ginger on plate.
5. Top with soy sauce.

> *Serves Four*

なすのしぎ焼き
NASU-SHIGIYAKI
Grilled Eggplant with Miso Paste

4 eggplants
sesame seed oil

*Special **Miso** Paste Sauce:*
  *½ cup red **miso** paste,*
  *½ cup **mirin**,*
  ½ cup sugar

white sesame seeds to
  taste

1. Cut eggplants in halves lengthwise.
2. Brush eggplants with sesame oil and grill until cooked.
3. Combine Special *Miso* Paste Sauce ingredients and cook over medium heat for 20 minutes.
4. Place eggplant on plate, top with Special Sauce and sesame seeds.

   Serves Four

揚げ出し豆腐
AGEDASHI-DOFU
Deep-Fried Tofu

*1½ packets **tofu***
oil for deep-frying
cornflour

***Tempura** Sauce:*
  *4 tablespoons **dashi**
  stock, 1 tablespoon soy
  sauce (low salt),
  1 tablespoon **mirin***

ground ginger to taste
bonito flakes
chopped spring onion

1. Drain **tofu** and cut into 8 pieces.
2. Heat oil to about 180°C.
3. Coat **tofu** with cornflour and fry for 5 minutes.
4. Heat **Tempura** Sauce.
5. Place **tofu**, ground ginger, bonito flakes and spring onion on flat plate.
6. Pour over hot **Tempura** Sauce.

   Serves Four

97

白酢あえ
SHIRASU-AE
Vegetable in Miso Paste

½ *piece* **konnyaku**

50g carrot

4 shiitake *mushrooms*

Special Sauce No. 1:
1 tablespoon **dashi**
stock, 1 tablespoon
mirin, *1 tablespoon*
light soy sauce

100g dried jelly fish

Special Sauce No. 2:
1 teaspoon vinegar,
1 teaspoon light soy
sauce, ½ teaspoon
sugar

½ *cucumber*

1 packet **tofu**

Special Sauce No. 3:
4 cups ground sesame
seeds, 3 tablespoons
sugar, 1 tablespoon
light soy sauce,
3 tablespoons vinegar

1. Cut **konnyaku**, carrot and **shiitake** into small pieces and cook in Special Sauce No. 1.
2. Cut jelly fish into small pieces and cover with hot water then cook in Special Sauce No. 2.
3. Shred cucumber and place in salted water.
4. Mash **tofu** and combine with Special Sauce No. 3.
5. Place vegetable, jelly fish and cucumber in bowl with **tofu** mixture.

Serves Four

いんげんのごま合え
INGEN NO GOMA-AE
Green Beans with Sesame Seeds

200g green beans

Marinade:
  ½ teaspoon **mirin**,
  ½ teaspoon soy sauce
  (low salt)

Special Sauce:
  4 cups ground sesame
  seeds, 1 tablespoon
  white sugar,
  1 tablespoon soy sauce
  (low salt), 2 cups
  dashi *stock*

1. Cut green beans into 3cm lengths.
2. Cook in boiling water for 2 minutes, drain.
3. Add beans to Marinade.
4. Combine Special Sauce ingredients.
5. Combine green bean mixture and Special Sauce, place in serving dish.

Serves Four

ブロッコリーの煮浸し
BUROKORI NO NIBITASHI
Broccoli

1 bunch broccoli
1 cup **dashi** *stock*
2 cups **sake**
3 cups soy sauce (low
   salt)

1. Cook broccoli in boiling water for 8 minutes.
2. Drain and leave to cool.
3. Heat remaining ingredients in a saucepan.
4. Add broccoli and cook for 5 minutes.
5. Leave in saucepan for a further 20 minutes before serving.

   Serves Four

ほうれん草の煮浸し
HORENSO NO NIBITASHI
Spinach

1 bunch spinach
1 piece deep-fried **tofu**

Special Sauce:
 1 cup **dashi**, *2 cups*
 soy sauce (low salt),
 1½ tablespoons **mirin**,
 1 teaspoon sugar

1. Pour boiling water over **tofu** to remove oil, cut into 3cm pieces.
2. Cook spinach in boiling water, drain and cut into 3cm pieces.
3. Heat Special Sauce ingredients.
4. Add spinach and **tofu** and cook for 5 minutes.
5. Leave for 20 minutes in saucepan before serving.

Serves Four

切り干し大根の煮つけ
KIRIBISHI-DAIKON
Dried White Radish in Soy Sauce

*50g dried **daikon** white
     radish*
*1 piece deep-fried **tofu***
1 cup water
*2 tablespoons **sake***
*4 tablespoons soy sauce
     (low salt)*
*1 small packet bonito
     flakes **katsuo***

1. Wash **daikon**, soak in water for 2 hours, drain and pat dry.
2. Pour hot water over deep-fried **tofu** to remove oil, cut into small pieces.
3. Place **daikon** and **tofu** in saucepan with 1 cup of water.
4. Cook for 3 minutes then add **sake** and soy sauce, cook for a further 7 minutes.
5. Place on plate with bonito flakes.

   Serves Four

れんこんとセロリのきんぴら
KINPIRA
Mixed Vegetables

> *200g lotus root* **renkon**, *chopped*
> *½ teaspoon vinegar*
> *1 cup water*
> *2 sticks celery*
> *1 tablespoon vegetable oil*
> *3 tablespoons soy sauce (low salt)*
> *3 tablespoons* **sake**
> *chili pepper to taste*
> *white sesame seeds to taste*

1. Mix vinegar in 1 cup of water and add chopped lotus root.
2. Boil celery and chop into small pieces.
3. Drain vegetables.
4. Heat oil in a pan and add vegetables.
5. Add soy sauce and **sake** and cook over high heat until sauce is absorbed.
6. Top with chili pepper and sesame seeds.

五目豆
GOMOKUMAME
Soy Beans and Vegetables

> 1 cup soy beans
> 5 cups water
> ½ **konnyaku**
> 3 **shiitake** mushrooms
> 10cm square **nori**
>   seaweed
> 70g carrot
> ½ cup sugar
> ¼ cup soy sauce (low
>   salt)

1. Wash soy beans and soak in water overnight.
2. Boil **konnyaku** and cut into small pieces.
3. Soften **shiitake** in water and cut into 1cm squares.
4. Cut **nori** and carrot into 1cm squares.
5. Cook soy beans over medium heat until soft.
6. Add vegetables and cook until soft.
7. Add sugar then soy sauce and cook over low heat until sauce is half-absorbed by vegetables (approximately 30 minutes).

Serves Four

みそだれおでん
ODEN
One-Pot Vegetables

*½ piece **daikon** white
radish*

*1 piece **konnyaku***

1 small carrot

8 small potatoes

*Special **Miso** Paste:
100g **miso** paste,
100g sugar*

*1 tablespoon ground
ginger*

*10cm square **nori**
seaweed*

*¼ cup soy sauce (low
salt)*

*¼ cup **sake***

4 eggs, hard-boiled

1. Cut daikon into 2cm pieces and boil.
2. Boil **konnyaku** and cut into 2cm pieces.
3. Boil carrot and potatoes and cut the carrot into 2cm lengths.
4. Heat Special **Miso** Paste ingredients in saucepan and mix until soft, add ground ginger.
5. Fill separate saucepan three-quarters full with water, add **nori**, soy sauce and **sake**.
6. Add **daikon, konnyaku**, eggs and potatoes and cook over low heat for 20 minutes.
7. Serve with Special **Miso** Paste as a dip for vegetables.

Serves Four

アボガドとトマトのからしあえ
AVOKADO TO TOMATO NO KARASHIAE
Avocado and Tomato Salad

> *1 avocado*
> *1 tomato*
>
> *Japanese mustard*
> *Dressing:*
> *1 tablespoon soy sauce*
> *(low salt),*
> *1 tablespoon lemon*
> *juice, 1 teaspoon mus-*
> *tard, ½ teaspoon sugar*
>
> *chopped **nori** seaweed,*
> *to taste*

1. Peel avocado and remove tomato skins and seeds.
2. Dice avocado and tomato.
3. Mix Dressing ingredients.
4. Pour Dressing over avocado and tomato pieces and top with **nori**.

> *Serves Four*

大根の一夜漬
DAIKON NO ICHIYA-ZUKE
White Radish

> *150g **daikon** white*
> *radish*
> *½ teaspoon salt*
> *1 lemon*
> *½ teaspoon black sesame*
> *seeds*
> *soy sauce (low salt), to*
> *taste*

1. Sprinkle salt on **daikon**.
2. Remove water with cloth.
3. Peel lemon and finely slice the rind.
4. Combine **daikon** with lemon rind and serve with black sesame seeds and soy sauce.

Serves Four

ダイコンと胡瓜のサラダ
DAIKON TO KYURI NO AEMONO
White Radish and Cucumber Salad

5cm **daikon** *white radish*
5cm *cucumber*
salt

Soy Sauce Dressing:
1 tablespoon light soy
sauce, 2 tablespoons
vegetable oil,
1 teaspoon sesame oil,
1 tablespoon white
vinegar

orange peel, chopped

1. Cut **daikon** and cucumber into thin strips.
2. Sprinkle with salt and allow to stand for 10 minutes to remove excess liquid.
3. Mix Soy Sauce Dressing ingredients.
4. Pour Dressing over **daikon** and cucumber and sprinkle with chopped orange peel.

   Serves Four

白菜とほうれん草の胡麻じょう油合え
HAKUSAI TO HORENSO NO GOMAJOYO AE
Chinese Cabbage and Spinach Salad

300g Chinese cabbage
150g spinach

Special Dressing:
 3 tablespoons ground sesame seeds,
 1½ tablespoons white sugar, 1½ tablespoons soy sauce (low salt)

1. Boil Chinese cabbage until soft and drain.
2. Boil spinach until soft and drain.
3. Spread cabbage leaves over bamboo mat, place the spinach in the middle and roll up.
4. Mix Special Dressing ingredients.
5. Cut the roll into four pieces.
6. Place the Dressing in a bowl and dip the rolls in before serving.

もやしと胡瓜のあえもの
MOYASHI TO KYURI NO AEMONO
Bean Shoots and Cucumber

100g bean shoots
100g cucumber
1 egg

Special Dressing:
    3 tablespoons soy
sauce (low salt),
    3 tablespoons white
vinegar, ½ teaspoon
sesame oil

10g ground ginger
3 spring onions, chopped

1. Place bean shoots in boiling water for 5 seconds, remove and allow to cool.
2. Cut cucumber into thin strips.
3. Combine Special Dressing ingredients and add ginger and spring onions.
4. Use the egg to make a thin omelette and cut into strips the same size as the cucumber.
5. Place cucumber, bean shoots and omelette in bowl and top with Dressing.

    Serves Four

もやしとうす揚げのごま味噌合え
MOYASHI TO USU AGE NO GOMAMISO-AE
Deep-Fried Tofu with Bean Shoots

200g bean shoots
1 piece of deep-fried **tofu**

Special Dressing:
4 tablespoons ground
sesame seeds,
2 tablespoons **miso**
paste, 3 teaspoons soy
sauce (low salt),
3 tablespoons vinegar,
1½ tablespoons sugar

1. Boil bean shoots for 5 minutes, remove and cool.
2. Grill **tofu** and cut into thin strips.
3. Combine Special Dressing ingredients.
4. Place bean shoots and **tofu** in bowl and top with Dressing.

   Serves Four

切り干し大根のあえもの
KIRIBOSHI DAIKON NO AEMONO
Dried White Radish Salad

50g *dried* **daikon** *white
  radish*

5cm pieces carrot

5cm **nori** *seaweed*

*Special Dressing:
  6 tablespoons white
  vinegar,
  2½ tablespoons sugar,
  1 tablespoon soy sauce
  (low salt)*

*½ tablespoon fresh lemon
  juice*

1 chili pepper

lemon peel, chopped

1. Soak dried **daikon** in cold water for 10 minutes.
2. Cut carrot and **nori** into long strips.
3. Combine Special Dressing ingredients.
4. Combine carrot, lemon juice and chili pepper.
5. Pour Dressing over top.
6. Serve with chopped lemon peel.

   Serves Four

白菜の漬物
HAKUSAI NO TSUKEMONO
Traditional Japanese Pickles

*1 large Chinese cabbage
(approx 2 kilo)*

*80g salt (40g per kilo
cabbage)*

10cm square **nori**
seaweed

3 chili peppers, chopped

1 cup **sake**

1. Cut Chinese cabbage into quarters and place in the sun for ½ a day to sweeten.
2. Place 1 tablespoon salt in a container and put in 2 matching sections of cabbage.
3. Sprinkle another tablespoon of salt on top.
4. Put in the 2 remaining cabbage quarters and sprinkle with remaining salt.
5. Place a weight on top (use a pickle stone or brick covered in foil).
6. After one day drain off the water.
7. Re-arrange cabbage as before, adding **nori**, chili pepper and **sake** between the 2 layers.
8. Place a weight on top and store for 3 days in a cool place.
9. Wash and cut each section into small pieces and serve with soy sauce (will keep for 2 weeks in fridge).

Note: Most popular in winter time

Serves Four

胡瓜の一夜漬
KYURI NO ICHIYA-ZUKE
Cucumber Pickle

> *4 pieces cucumber*
> *salt*
> *1 cup* **moromi** *sweet rice*
> *paste*
> *3 tablespoons* **mirin**

1. Wash cucumber and sprinkle with salt, allow to stand for 30 minutes.
2. Cut cucumber into 2cm lengths.
3. Mix **moromi** and **mirin** till soft.
4. Combine cucumber and **moromi** paste and allow to stand for 40 minutes.

   Serves Four

なすの一夜漬
NASU NO ICHIYA ZUKE
Eggplant Pickle

2 eggplants
2 green peppers
salt
*10cm square **kobu** (kelp)*

Special Soy Sauce:
  3 tablespoons soy
  sauce (low salt),
  *1½ tablespoons **mirin**,*
  *1 tablespoon **dashi***
  stock

chili pepper to taste

1. Remove tops from eggplants and cut in half.
2. Place in salted water for 1 hour, drain and chop into small pieces.
3. Cut into 2cm lengths.
4. Chop green pepper into small pieces.
5. Mix green pepper, eggplant and salt in a bowl until soft.
6. Squeeze vegetables in a cloth to remove water.
7. Combine Special Soy Sauce ingredients.
8. Combine Special Sauce, vegetables and **kobu** and allow to stand for 30 minutes.
9. Place vegetables on a plate with chili pepper on top.

   Serves Four

美しいごちそう

Japanese Favourites

Japanese Favourites

In Japanese favourites there are recipes for some of the more famous international Japanese dishes, such as **tempura, tonkatsu, sukiyaki** and **teppanyaki**. Other popular dishes such as the Japanese lunch box **makunouchi**, the Japanese Dim Sims **ebe shumai** and the Japanese favourite pancake **okonomiyaki**, that are not part of the formal menus, are included. Finally ways of serving Japan's national drinks, green tea and **sake**, are described.

すき焼き
SUKIYAKI
Beef with Vegetables

Sukiyaki is a Japanese favourite one-pot dish **nabemono** that is cooked at the table.

Top quality Japanese beef such as Matsuzaka or Kobe is said to be the most tasty and tender beef and also the most expensive in the world. These cows drink beer, have daily massages and are fed grains and other nutritional food.

Traditionally Japanese did not eat meat. In the seventh century, Buddhism was declared the national religion and the killing of animals was prohibited. After the Meiji Restoration in 1868 Japan introduced Western culture and *sukiyaki* was encouraged as a way of eating beef. It was a very different way of eating as it meant breaking the religious taboo of individual bowls and chopsticks to sharing food from the same container. For this same reason *nabemono* is not served as part of a formal dinner, nor are chopsticks mixed together. This was based on an ancient religious belief about personality being transmitted through the chopsticks and that they should be only used by one person and then thrown away.

800g scotch fillet, sliced
2 pieces **tofu**
400g Chinese cabbage
200g vermicelli
oil for cooking

Sukiyaki *Sauce:*
  1 cup soy sauce (low salt), 1 cup sugar,
  1 cup **mirin**, *2 cups* **dashi** *stock*

100g bamboo shoots
40g **shiitake** *mushrooms*
1 bunch spring onions
4 eggs, beaten

1. Cut **tofu** into 2cm squares.
2. Cut Chinese cabbage into 4cm squares.
3. Place vermicelli in boiling water for 10 minutes then cut into 10cm lengths.
4. Place oil in electric frypan and heat to high.
5. Place the beef in the frypan and fry for approximately 3 minutes.
6. Add the **Sukiyaki** Sauce ingredients and vegetables.
7. Serve from frypan at table and then dip pieces in beaten egg.

Serves Four

天ぷら
TEMPURA
Fried Seafood and Vegetables

The origin of the word ***tempura*** comes from the Portuguese Jesuits in Nagasaki in the 17th Century. This was their term for the days on which they only ate fish and not meat.

Appetising yet easy to prepare, ***tempura*** is made by dipping small pieces of fish and/or vegetables into a batter of flour and iced water then quickly deep frying them in vegetable oil.

Some useful hints for preparing this dish include making sure all ingredients are dry before frying. Leave making the batter until the last minute and keep it a bit lumpy rather than overbeating it. ***Tempura*** is usually served with soup, rice, pickles and ***sake*** or tea.

8 whiting fillets

8 prawns, shelled and deveined

200g pumpkin

40g carrot

40g sweet potato

40g green beans

40g green pepper

Tempura *Batter:*
130g plain flour, 1 egg yolk, 1½ cups of cold water

oil for deep-frying

Tempura *Sauce:*
4 tablespoons **dashi**
stock, 1 tablespoon
soy sauce (low salt),
1 tablespoon **mirin**

10g ground ginger
20g ground **daikon**

1. Peel pumpkin, carrot and potato and chop into 8mm pieces.
2. Cut green beans into 3cm pieces and thread onto toothpicks, three pieces on each.
3. Remove seeds from green pepper and cut into 2cm pieces.
4. Heat oil to 170°C.
5. Roll fish and prawns in flour, dip in ***Tempura*** Batter and cook for 2 minutes.
6. Dip vegetables in Batter and cook for 3 minutes.
7. Place fish and vegetables on a plate.
8. Serve with ***Tempura*** Sauce, ginger and radish.

トンカツ
TONKATSU
Deep Fried Pork

Tonkatsu is one of the most popular meat dishes in Japan. It is usually served on a bed of shredded cabbage with a bowl of rice, pickles, tea and a dipping sauce.

Tonkatsu first appeared in Japan in the Meiji era (1868-1912). There is some dispute as to whether its origins are Japanese or European. The name of this dish is formed from the Chinese ton (pig) and **katsu,** an abbreviation of the English cutlet.

> *4 pieces pork loin*
> *salt and pepper*
> * (optional)*
> *1 cup plain flour*
> *1 egg, beaten*
> *1 cup breadcrumbs*
> *oil for deep-frying*
> *80g cabbage, shredded*
> *1 lemon, sliced*
> *English mustard*
>
> **Tonkatsu** *Sauce:*
> * 4 tablespoons of*
> * Worcestershire sauce,*
> * 4 tablespoons tomato*
> * juice, sesame seeds to*
> * taste*

1. Score the pork and sprinkle with salt and pepper (optional).
2. Roll in flour, dip in egg and coat with breadcrumbs.
3. Deep-fry pork for 3 minutes in oil heated to about 170°C.
4. Place the pork on plate with cabbage, lemon, mustard and **Tonkatsu** Sauce.

Serves Four

幕の内
MAKUNOUCHI
Lunch Box

*T*he **makunouchi** lunchbox is a take-away meal presented in a decorative box or basket. Ideal for travelling, picnics, or watching the sumo wrestling.

The typical lunch box is divided into four sections reserved for raw fish, fried dishes, vegetables/pickles/salad/omelettes and steamed rice.

It is a collection of many taste-tempting assorted dishes. For instance at Kyoto Restaurant the food selection includes:

> **Sashimi**
>
> **Tempura**
>
> **Yakitori**
>
> *Deep Fried Prawns*
>
> *Cooked Vegetables*
>
> *Pickles*
>
> *Omelette*
>
> *Steamed Rice*
>
> *Salad*

お好み焼
OKONOMIYAKI
Japanese Savoury Pancakes

These are a favourite snack meal for the Japanese. The pancakes are usually cooked at the table in a frypan and eaten immediately. **Konomi** roughly translated means 'choice or taste' or whatever you like or have in the refrigerator. This could be strips of pork or chicken, prawns and seaweed. There are many restaurants that specialise in serving **okonomiyaki**. Its origins can be traced back to the Edo period (1615-1868) as a form of pancake that was offered at certain Buddhist ceremonies. Its popularity spread after the Great Kanto Earthquake in 1923 when food was scarce and residents in Tokyo and Yokohama used whatever food scraps were available.

150g flour

¼ teaspoon salt (optional)

¼ teaspoon baking powder

*²/₃ cup **dashi** stock*

100g meat or fish

200g cabbage

*4 **shiitake** mushrooms*

vegetable oil for frying

4 eggs

Special Sauce:
Combine 6 tablespoons Japanese Worcestershire sauce, 2 tablespoons tomato sauce and 1 teaspoon whisky

1. Sift flour, salt and baking powder in a large bowl.
2. Gradually add *dashi* stock.
3. Cut meat or fish into small pieces, shred cabbage, slice mushrooms and divide these ingredients among 4 bowls.
4. Heat electric frypan to 250°C, add oil.
5. Divide batter into 4 portions and place in bowls.
6. Break egg into each bowl and mix well with batter.
7. Spoon mixture into heated frypan to form a pancake 1cm thick and 15cm wide.
8. When pancake is half-cooked turn and fry the other side.
9. Serve with Special Sauce.
10. Repeat steps 7-10, 3 more times.

Serves Four

海老シューマイ
EBE SHUMAI
Japanese Dim Sim

This is a very popular lunch-time take-away snack available from railway stations. The most famous *shumai* Restaurant is Kiyoken in Yokohama and serves many different varieties. Japanese dim sims are Chinese based but use different ingredients.

300g shrimps
*2 **shiitake** mushrooms*

Seasoning:
1 tablespoon sugar,
1 tablespoon soy sauce
(low salt), 1 teaspoon
sesame oil, 1 teaspoon
pepper

300g pork mince
3 tablespoons cornflour
*20 sheets **shumai** skin*

1. Wash shrimps in salted water, dry and cut into small pieces.
2. Soak **shiitake** in water, drain and remove stalks.
3. Combine Seasoning ingredients.
4. Add prawns and mix by hand.
5. Add pork mince, cornflour and mushrooms, mix together all ingredients.
6. Place 1/20th of the mixture on each **shumai** wrapper, roll up and seal.
7. Steam **shumai** for about 13 minutes over high heat.

Serves Four: 20 Pieces

Tea

*J*apanese drink their tea green, unlike the Indians, who allow the tea leaves to dry and ferment, going a blackish, brown colour. Green tea is always drunk without milk or sugar, although it is often served with little tea cakes. Its origins go back to where the Buddhist Monks brewed this beverage to help them stay awake at night, to say their prayers. It was also thought to have strong medicinal value and a Japanese Priest Esui offered it to the Shogun to cure his hangover! The Tea Ceremony has its origins in Zen Buddhism and has developed over the centuries as a specialised Japanese art form, where the etiquette of the tearoom and its environment have been embodied in a philosophy that has had a significant impact on Japanese thought and protocol. Many interesting books have been written on the Tea Ceremony and are worth reading to increase your knowledge about Japanese philosophy, art and culture.

The tea that is used in the formal Tea Ceremony *chanoyu* is expensive powdered tea. For everyday use, leaf tea with various grades are used depending on the occasion, **bancha** for restaurants and *sencha* for drinking at home. Tea should be bought a little at a time and stored in a cool dark container for no more than a few months.

It is the custom to drink tea not during but after a meal to assist digestion, usually with the last course of rice and pickles.

To Make Japanese Tea

Bancha

Bancha is the lowest grade but most commonly used, usually being served free in Japanese restaurants. It is now available in instant tea-bags.

1. Warm the pot with hot water.
2. Place 3 teaspoons of **bancha** leaves in the pot.
3. Add 3 cups of boiling water.
4. Let stand for 3 minutes.
5. Pour into cups.

Makes 5 cups

Do not let tea stand or brew. Empty pot and use fresh leaves for another round.

Sake

Sake is Japan's national alcoholic drink, made from fermented rice. It is very high in alcohol, in fact 15-17% (beer 3-4%); no wonder it is always served in small cups!

Sake has no vintage years, in fact it is better drunk within the year it is bottled. Good **sake** depends on the quality of the rice and the purity of the water (similar to scotch).

Tokkyu is special class, **Ikkyu** first class and **Nikyu** second class. In making liquor from grain, starch must be converted into saccharoid. While the western world uses malt for this purpose, Asian countries have developed fermentation techniques using mould. In Japan it is called **koji** a yellow mould cultured on steamed rice. When the rice and **koji** mixture is placed in a cloth bag after fermentation and squeezed out, the sake lees (sediment) and liquid separate, yielding a clear liquor. **Sake** made in ancient times and even today brewed at home has a white liquor containing grains of rice called **doburoku**. Home-brewing is now prohibited.

To Prepare Sake

Sake is usually warmed in small ceramic flasks and drunk out of tiny ceramic cups. The normal procedure is to place the flasks containing the **sake** into hot water. It should not be overheated, about 45°-50°C for 5 minutes and should never be allowed to boil. Heating sake brings out its fragrance and mellowness.

How To Drink Sake

Formal etiquette requires people not to pour their own **sake**. So it is considered polite for you to fill the other persons cup and vice versa.

This custom has its origins in the ancient religious festivals where the **sake** was offered to the Shinto god and then shared in turn by every other person in order of rank.

Glossary of Japanese Ingredients, Cooking Methods, and Utensils

A

Abura-Age (deep-fried tofu)

Tofu is sliced thinly, cut to a fixed size, its water removed, then it is deep fried in oil. There is a thin *usu-age* and a thick type *atsu-age*. *Abura-age* refers to the thin type. Before using, hot water is poured over it, and the excess oil on the surface is wiped off. It is used as an ingredient in various types of cooking, such as boiled dishes, *miso* soup, and rice dishes.

Aemono

Mixed things such as poultry, fish and vegetables in a sauce or dressing. It is a type of salad that accompanies a main dish.

Agar-Agar

A pure form of gelatine processed from a type of red seaweed called *tengusa*. In Japanese cooking, agar-agar is used for sweets and confections. One of its valuable properties is that it sets without refrigeration, at 42°C to 30°C, sealing in the freshness of fruits and other foods.

Agemono

Deep fried foods, including *tempura*.

Aji (horse mackerel)

The varieties of aji are extremely numerous. Its distinctive characteristic is hard scales beginning directly under the head and extending to the tail. It is used for *tataki sashimi*.

Aji-Ni-Moto, MSG (monosodium glutamate)

Powder used to enhance flavour. It should be used, as the Japanese do, very sparingly. It may be omitted, if preferred, from any recipe.

Aka-Togarashi (red pepper)

There are two major groups, sweet and hot. The hot type, the one most generally used as seasoning, is called **aka-togarashi**. The pods of red peppers are green when young but turn red when they mature. The dried pods are used in cooking, but since the seeds are very hot, they are taken out and the pod is cut up. These are added as hot flavouring to pickled and boiled vegetables.

Amazu-Shoga

Pickled ginger without extra colouring. It has a light pink colour.

Aonoriko

Powdered green laver, a member of the seaweed family, used as a seasoning agent.

Aoyagi (trough shells)

These are the foot portion of the trough shell. It is seldom sold in the shell. The shell ligament, excluding the foot, is highly priced as a delicacy. The foot portion is used for **sashimi** and as an ingredient for vinegared dishes, such as **sunomono** and **sushi**.

Asari (short-necked clams)

They are used in their shell for soups and are also cooked with rice wine. When shelled, they are used in dishes such as **nuta** (a side dish of shell-fish, **wakame** and long green onions with vinegared **miso**), **zosui** (a porridge of rice and vegetables), and in **nabemono** (one-pot table cooking).

Asatsuki (chives)

This variety of **negi** resembles chives in appearance. Eaten when it reaches a length of 10-15cm, it is a delicate onion with mild flavour and fragrance. It is cut finely and used as a condiment and to add colouring to soups.

Azuki (red beans)

Small red beans are the most frequently used legume in Japanese cooking besides soy beans. They are steamed with glutinous rice for special occasions, or more commonly, boiled with sugar to make sweet red bean paste, which forms the basis of a large percentage of Japanese sweets and confections.

131

B

Buri (yellowtail)

This fish is a spindle shape, and in the centre of its body is one yellow stripe. Those over 1 metre long are especially delicious. It is very good salted, coated with **teriyaki** sauce and grilled or boiled with flavourings. The young fish, called **hamachi**, is extremely delicious as **sashimi**.

C

Chawan-Mushi

A tall, straight-sided lidded soup pot for cooking **chawan-mushi**, a savoury steamed custard.

D

Daikon (long white radish)

This white root grows rather large compared with other varieties. It is used primarily in boiled dishes and for pickling, grating, marinating, or as condiment for **sashimi**.

Daizu (soy beans)

May be eaten as a fresh vegetable or selected for drying; they are also used to make soy sauce, **miso** paste and **tofu**. A rich source of first class protein, they make an excellent substitute for meat in many dishes.

Dashi

This is hot water flavoured with **konbu** (kelp) and flakes of bonito **katsuobushi**, which are strained out before the **dashi** is used.

Dashi No Moto (instant **dashi**)

This is a basic soup and cooking stock available in packets made from powdered **katsuobushi** and **kombu**.

Donabe

This is a lidded earthenware casserole unglazed outside, glazed inside. Comes in various sizes and can be used over direct heat. The larger sizes are used for one-pot dishes cooked at the table, such as simmered beef and vegetables **shabu-shabu**. Any fireproof casserole can be used.

Donburi

A large individual ceramic bowl, often with lid, used for noodle and rice dishes.

E

Ebi (shrimp or prawns)

There are many varieties, but the one most commonly eaten in Japan is the tiger prawn.

Enokitake (mushrooms)

These have slender, long, yellow stems topped by tiny round caps. Mild in flavour, they retain a certain crispness and aroma when cooked in soups and one-pot dishes.

F

Fu

Light cake made of wheat gluten, available in packets in different sizes, shapes and colours. Used principally as a soup garnish.

G

Gen-En-Shoyu

Low salt soy sauce. ·

Ginnan (ginkgo nuts)

Several layers of the kernel must be removed before a smooth white nut is exposed. This is prized for its delicate flavour and attractive colour and included in many steamed, grilled and deep-fried dishes. Ginkgo nuts may be purchased fresh or canned.

Gobo (burdock)

A long, slender, irregularly shaped root vegetable whose crunchy texture and ability to absorb the flavours of simmering juices and sauces make it an essential ingredient of Japanese cuisine. Fresh burdock should be trimmed, washed and scrubbed with a brush, but not peeled. After slicing, it should be immersed in cold water so that its colour is retained. Oriental speciality grocers generally carry both the fresh root and a pre-parboiled, canned variety, not peeled. After slicing, it should be immersed in cold water so that its colour is retained.

Goma (sesame seeds)

These are the flattish seeds of the sesame herb. There are 3 types distinguished by colour — black, white and brown. With the black variety, the seeds are large and the yield high, but their quality and oil content are comparatively low. With the white variety the seeds are small and yield low, but quality is high. They, therefore, measure up better as food than do the black ones. Brown sesame seeds are similar to the black ones. The type of seed used and the way it is used varies according to the type of dish. The seeds are used whole or lightly toasted and ground.

Goma-Abura (sesame seed oil)

Made from sesame seeds, which are rich in oil and protein, this oil has a unique taste and aroma. It is mixed with salad oil and used for frying *tempura* or used to add flavour and aroma to Japanese-style dressed dishes *aemono*.

H

Hakusai (Japanese cabbage)

This large, leafy vegetable is pale green at the top of the crinkle-edged leaves and creaming-white at the stem, where stalks are thick and tender. It is mild, almost sweet, with a more pronounced flavour than lettuce. It is simmered, used in one-pot dishes and in soups, pickles and salads..

Hakusai (Chinese cabbage)

This has smooth white stalks and large green leaves. Will keep for one week refrigerated in a plastic bag. Substitute celery or white cabbage.

Hamaguri (clams)

Clams are often served on special occasions such as weddings. Clams in their shells are used for soups. When removed from their shells, they are typically grilled or boiled in rice wine.

Hashi (chopsticks)

These are used for both eating and cooking. Cooking chopsticks are usually made of wood or bamboo, of various lengths up to about 30cm, with small holes at the top ends so that they can be tied loosely together in pairs with kitchen string. Eggs are stirred with chopsticks instead of being beaten, and chopsticks are used to turn foods when frying and for mixing foods together, taking the place of cooking spoons and forks. Five or six chopsticks, held in a bunch in the right hand, are used to stir certain dishes.

Chopsticks for the table may be made of wood or bamboo, plain or lacquered, plastic, ivory and sometimes metal. In Japanese shops 20cm bamboo chopsticks are sold in joined pairs in individual paper wrapping and must be broken apart for use. Almost all Japanese food is eaten with chopsticks of this type. They can, of course, be washed and re-used.

Hibachi

Japanese charcoal grill available in various sizes. Can be used indoors or out.

Hich Mi Togarashi

Seven-pepper spice, available in small bottles. Powdered blend of hot mustard seed, sesame seed, pepper leaf, poppy seed, rape seed, hemp seed and dried tangerine peel.

Hijiki

Flaked dried seaweed that looks rather like dry tea leaves but which expands by as much as four or five times in liquid.

Horenso (spinach)

Japanese spinach has small leaves, a delicate flavour and a tender stem in comparison to the spinach sold here. Choose very young, tender spinach as a substitute.

Hotategai (scallops)

The shell ligament is large and soft, but becomes tough when overcooked. When very fresh, they are used for *sashimi*, but can be grilled in the shell over direct heat or shelled and grilled with *teriyaki* sauce.

Hyamugi

Thin noodles, usually eaten cold. A substitute is Italian vermicelli.

I

Ika (squid)

The most commonly eaten in Japan is the *surume-ika*. Because it has little oil, the taste is simple and light. There are many cooking methods ranging from *sashimi* to boiling, grilling, and deep frying. When preparing, it is necessary to avoid overcooking or it will become tough. Squid is also processed in dried form and is sometimes salted and pickled.

Iwashi (sardines)

Iwashi are characterised by a line of black spots on either side of their bodies. They also have a large number of small bones. Among the varieties, *ma-iwashi* is the most delicious. When boiled, soy sauce and fresh ginger are added to kill the fishy smell. If very fresh, they are used for *sashimi*. Canned sardines packed in oil are processed products using varieties of *Iwashi*.

J

Jaga-Imo (potatoes)

Two main varieties are used in Japan, both of which are thin skinned and relatively small. Sweet potatoes are also used in small quantities.

K

Kabo-Cha (pumpkin)

Most have a flat, globular shape and look like a cross between a small Western pumpkin and a variety of hard-skinned squash. Their meat is fleshy and highly palatable. It is boiled with seasonings or slices and deep fried. Flesh is bright yellow, has a rich flavour and is pleasantly smooth textured. It can be cut into bite sized pieces and simmered, or sliced and deep fried as a *tempura* vegetable. It can also be sculpted in an elaborate centrepiece for a banquet or other festive occasions.

Kaki (persimmons)

Best when purchased fresh and firm, they are peeled before use and typically served as a desert at a Japanese dinner. Iced *kaki* (sherbet) or dried *hushi kaki* are good to serve at afternoon tea.

Kamaboko (fish paste)

This is made by adding a starchy binding agent to pureed white fish, moulding the mixture into shape, then steaming it. It is sold in 175g cakes. *Kamaboko* is an important ingredient in *oden* and other stews.

Kampyo

Dried strips of the winter melon, also called dried gourd strips, used for tying various foods.

Kana-Gushi

Long and short metal skewers used for grilling many types of food, including whole fish.

Karashii (mustard)

The dry, ground mustard used in Japan is very fiery and should be used sparingly. Made into a paste with a little water it is used in dipping sauces, pot dishes and salad dressings.

Katakuriko

Flour made from the root of the Japanese dog-toothed violet, closely resembles arrowroot, used to thicken sauces and as a coating for foods.

Katsuo-Bushi (bonito flakes)

Fillets of the bonito, a member of the mackerel family, are dried to make a solid block of bonito. The finest **dashi** is made with flakes shaved from this solid block. However, the difficulty of obtaining a bonito block, and the skill required to 'shave' it, make pre-flaked bonito more convenient. Packaged dried bonito flakes are called **hana-katsuo**.

Kikurage (cloud ear mushrooms)

Often labelled 'dried black fungus', these look more like chips of wrinkled bark or dried seaweed than mushrooms. The dried form must be reconstituted in tepid water for 20 minutes before use. They are added to numerous savoury dishes.

Kinako

Soy bean flour.

Kinugoshi Tofu

Silky bean curd, a custard-like cake made from white soy beans, sold fresh from the refrigerator section of health food shops and sometimes from supermarkets. Will keep for several days if put into a container with water that is changed daily. This is a more delicate form of bean curd than **momen tofu**, often called cotton bean curd.

Kinome

A general term for young leaves, that are used widely as garnishes in Japanese cooking. The fragrant sprig of the sansho tree is particularly popular, both as a garnish and for seasoning.

Kishimen

Broad, flat, wheat-flour noodles.

Kisu (sillago)

Its meat is white and soft and because its flavour is light it is a fish with a broad range of cooking methods. It is a main ingredient for *tempura*.

Kome (uncooked rice)

In the Japanese diet, rice is a staple food served at every mealtime. Throughout the areas of the world, a large number of varieties of rice are cultivated. Distinguished by shape of kernel, the Japanese form is short and roundish, while slim long rice is the most common form outside Asia. Rice can be divided into glutinous and non-glutinous types according to the difference in nature of the kernel's starch, which is the principal ingredient of rice. In Japan, non-glutinous wet-land rice is used almost exclusively.

Konbu (dried kelp)

This dark greenish-brown sea vegetable is an important flavouring agent for *dashi*. The white mould that lightly dusts its surface contributes to its sweetish flavour, and should not be rubbed or washed away. *Konbu* is sold dried, in cellophane packs. Dried *konbu* may be stored at room temperature in a dry airtight container. *Konbu* that has been reserved from making *dashi* will keep 3 or 4 days in a refrigerator, tightly covered with a plastic wrap.

Konnyaku

This gelatinous, pearly grey cake is processed from the root of a vegetable called 'Devil's Tongue'. Like *tofu* and burdock, it has little taste of its own, but absorbs liquids and their flavours readily. It is sometimes labelled 'yam cake'.

Kuri (chestnuts)

There are two main varieties — *Tamba* are large, firm and well textured and *shiba* are small, firm and sweet. Chestnuts can be bought fresh, canned or preserved in a thick syrup and are used in many Japanese sweet and savoury dishes.

Kushi

Small bamboo or metal skewers, available in Japanese shops.

Kuzu (starch)

An all-purpose thickener for soups and stews, this starch is extracted from the root of the **kuzu** vine, a wild plant which is very common in Japan. **Kuzu** starch not only give soups and stews a glossy 'finish', it is also a fine coating for deep-fried foods. It is expensive, however, and cornflour can be substituted.

Kuzu Shirataki

Dried green bean noodles, sometimes used in **sukiyaki** instead of **shirataki**.

Kyuri (cucumber)

Japanese cucumbers are smaller, have a much clearer flavour and are less watery than the larger varieties.

Kyuri Narazuke

Nara-style pickled cucumber.

M

Maguro (tuna)

Most of the varieties of tuna are large. 'Black tuna' or **kuromaguro** is the variety most commonly eaten fresh in Japan, the name coming from the blue-black lines on its back. The type used for canned tuna is a different variety. Fresh tuna is grilled or boiled, but its most general use is for **sashimi**. Also, tuna is hardly ever omitted as an ingredient for **sushi**. The value of the cut depends on the part of the fish from which it comes. The part valued most highly is the section around the stomach called toro which contains a lot of oil.

Matsutake (mushrooms)

Scented with the fragrance of pine forests these are only very lightly cooked to retain their unique aroma. **Matsutake** are one of the most sought-after delicacies in Japan and are as highly prized as truffles are by the French. **Matsutake** are never dried and rarely canned.

Mirin (sweet rice wine for cooking)

This is a type of alcohol made from sweet glutinous short-grained rice **mochi-gome** and known as **honmirin**. Its alcohol content ranges between 13 to 22 per cent and its sugar content between 25 and 38 per cent. The combination of alcohol and sugar gives **mirin** a distinctive flavour and sweetness. **Mirin** is never used for drinking; it is used primarily to add sweet flavour to cooking, such as to boiled or grilled dishes or to add taste and sheen.

Miso

Paste made from fermented, cooked soy beans. Two main types, **aka miso** (red bean paste) and **shiro miso** (white bean paste), are available in vacuum-sealed plastic bags. When **miso** appears in a recipe without specifying red or white **miso**, either may be used.

Misozuke

Meat, fish, or vegetables pickled in bean paste.

Mitsuba (trefoil)

This herb, a member of the parsley family, appears frequently in Japanese cuisine. Used either coarsely chopped, or whole, it is added both for its flavour and its decorative green colour.

Mochi (glutinous rice cakes)

Heavy and substantial, these are made by pounding piping hot glutinous rice into mounds or cakes of various sizes. They can be purchased fresh, factory packed or vacuum packed in plastic. Served grilled and accompanied by a dipping sauce or a wrapping of toasted seaweed, they are usually eaten on festive occasions.

Mochigome (sticky, sweet, glutinous rice)
A short-grained rice that sticks together when cooked.

Momen Tofu
Sometimes called cotton bean curd, it is custard-like cake made from white soy beans, sold fresh from the refrigerator section of health food shops. Water should be changed daily.

Momiji-Oroshi
This is made by stuffing a slice of Japanese white radish **daikon** with dried, hot, red chilies, then grating them together. The resultant mix of red and white is said to look like maple leaves turning in autumn.

N

Nabemono (one-pot cookery)
An electric frying-pan or a fireproof earthenware casserole **donabe**, heavy frying-pan, or shallow, round, cast-iron pot **sukiyaki-nabe** on an electric or other type of table heater, or a charcoal-burning **hibachi** can all be used for these dishes, where the food is cooked at the table.

Nagashikan
An aluminium loaf tin with inserted sideless tray that lifts out, making it easy to remove and slice custards and similar dishes that would be hard to unmould.

Namaudon
Fresh noodles, ready-cooked in 200g packages needing only to be reheated in hot water. Also uncooked **namaudon**, to be cooked in the same way as dry noodles.

Nameko
Tiny button mushrooms that are generally sold canned for use in soups and one-pots.

Naruto-Maki
A popular fish sausage, which has a spiral pattern of pink or yellow running through it.

Nashi (pears)
Japanese pears are apple-like in shape and texture, yellow to brown in colour.

Nasu (eggplant)

All Japanese eggplants are smaller than those found in the West. The most common variety is sweeter and less watery than the Western aubergine; the small aubergines available in Asian food shops can be substituted.

Natto

Fermented soy beans, eaten as a garnish with rice.

Negi (long onion)

There are two main types. One **ha-negi,** most of which is green, has cylindrical leaves and stem and is eaten primarily for its green part. The other **nebuka-negi,** the major part of which is white, has hard leaves and is eaten primarily for the white stem part. It is slightly smaller in diameter but more pithy than a leek. Both types are used in the same way — as an ingredient for **sukiyaki** and other one-pot table cooking **nabemono** and as a condiment for soups and noodle dishes.

Nimono

Simmered foods cooked in a number of differently flavoured stocks. Meats, poultry, fish and vegetables are all cooked by this method.

Nori (seaweed)

This is the most common of the many varieties of seaweed that the Japanese consume. **Nori,** often translated as 'laver', is used as a **sushi**-wrap and a garnish for many dishes. Dried **nori** should be freshened by a light toasting.

O

Oroshi-Gane

A very fine grater made of aluminium or ceramic with a well at the end for collecting juices. This is ideal for grating ginger for juice and for grating white radish, *daikon*.

Oshiwaku

An oblong wooden box about 15 x 10cm, with a removable top and bottom, used for pressing vinegared rice when making certain kinds of *sushi*.

P

Ponzu (pon vinegar)

Made from *dai dai*, a lime-like Japanese citrus fruit. Use lime or lemon juice as a substitute, though they will lack the fragrance of *ponzu*.

R

Renkon (lotus root)

This crunchy vegetable appears in *tempura*, vinegared and simmered dishes. Generally cut into rounds, it has an attractive flower-like cross section. As it discolours quickly after paring, it should be kept in a dish of lightly vinegared cold water until used.

S

Saba (mackerel)

Its taste is rich, and its meat oily. This fish has a good flavour when boiled or grilled, especially when boiled with *miso* paste and fresh ginger.

Sake (salmon)

The whole fish from head to tail can be put to many uses, such as grilling or cooking in stock-based dishes. Additionally, the eggs which are pickled in salt are prized very highly. These are called *ikura* and are used for *sushi*.

Sake (rice wine)

Usually called **nihon-shu** (Japanese wine) or **sake**, it is brewed using rice as the major ingredient and has an alcoholic content of 15 to 17 per cent. **Sake** is divided into 3 grades — special **tokkyu**, first **ikkyu** and second **nikyu**. It is used mainly as an alcoholic drink, but for seasoning food, second grade **sake** is commonly employed. Used similarly to sweet cooking **sake mirin**, to give flavour to boiled and sauteed dishes.

Sansai

A seasonal variety of bracken which is pickled and served with noodles.

Sansho (prickly-ash powder)

This spice, made by grinding the small yellowish seed-pods of the prickly ash tree, is unique to Japan.

Sashimi

Slices of raw fish, served with garnishes.

Sato-Imo Taro

Available fresh or tinned in Japanese markets as **sato-imo**, they are sometimes called Japanese potatoes. They look like medium-sized potatoes with a rough brown skin marked by prominent rings.

Satsuma-Age (sweet potato)

One of the white or yellow-fleshed varieties.

Saya-Endo (snow peas)

Snow peas are one variety of shell pea with edible shell. The shells are small, smooth and glossy, juicy and soft. After the strings have been removed and they are cooked in boiling water, snow peas are dressed *ohitashi*, added to Japanese-style side dishes *aemono*, or used as garnishing dishes boiled with flavourings *nimono*.

Schichimi-Togarashi (seven flavour cayenne)

This is a seasoning powder made from ground hot red chillies, ground Japanese pepper leaf, sesame, mustard, rape and poppy seeds, and dried tangerine peel. Sold in containers to be used as an on-the-table condiment. It is used sparingly to season noodle dishes, in one-pot table cookery, and for *yakitori*.

Seri

Belonging to the same family as celery, it is a kind of parsley. Flat parsley is the best substitute.

Shamoji

A round wooden spatula used for stirring and serving rice. It does not break up the rice grains.

Shiitake (Chinese black mushroom)

These mushrooms are sold raw or dried; the dried ones are better in flavour and aroma. The raw ones are used for steamed dishes, in one-pot table cooking *nabemono* and soup.

Shirataki

Translucent, jelly-like noodles. These are thin filaments made by shredding *konnyaku*. They are used mainly as an ingredient for one-pot dishes boiled at the table *nabemono* or in dressed dishes *aemono*.

Shirataki (translucent noodles)

Made from the roots of the Devil's Tongue, called *konnyaku* in Japan. Available water-packed in tins or vacuum-sealed plastic bags.

Shiratama-Ko (rice cake flour)

Shiso (leaves of the beefsteak plant)

There are two types — one with purple-red leaves **aka-jiso** and another with green leave **ao-jiso**. The green variety is the one most commonly used in cooking. The leaf is cut finely and mixed with rice or with pickled vegetables, or is served whole as a complement to **sashimi**.

Shoga (fresh ginger)

The edible part of the plant is the root. It has a strong flavour and smell, used both as a seasoning and condiment. Pickled ginger shoots **ha-shoga** are served as a complement to grilled fish and other dishes, while fully grown ginger root **ne-shoga** is cut into needle-fine strips or grated in dishes boiled with flavourings **nimono**. It is always served together with **sushi** and certain **tofu** dishes as condiment.

Shoyu (soy sauce)

This is the basic liquid seasoning used in Japanese cooking. There are many varieties, but the most commonly used are **koi-kuchi-shoyu** (regular soy sauce) and **usu-kuchi-shoyu** (light-coloured soy sauce). By far the most popular brand in Japan is Kikkoman. **Koi-kuchi-shoyu** (regular Kikkoman Soy Sauce) is the most versatile. It has a deep reddish-brown colour, a rich, complex flavour and a savoury aroma. These characteristics are achieved by using equal parts of soybeans and wheat in the mash, and a fermentation period of more than 6 months under careful microbial control to encourage enzyme action to mature the mash completely. **Gen-En-Shoyu** (Kikkoman Milder Soy Sauce) is a low-salt soy sauce brewed in the traditional way to give it the flavour of regular Kikkoman Soy Sauce. Then, about 43% of the salt is removed. Its use need not be limited to those who must reduce their sodium consumption. It is recommended for use as a recipe ingredient as well as a table condiment. **Usu-kuchi-shoyu** (Kikkoman Light Colour Soy Sauce) is brewed similarly to regular Kikkoman Soy Sauce but under stricter controls to reduce the intensity of the colour. The result is about one-fourth the colour of regular soy sauce. It is used where it is not desirable to darken the natural colour of ingredients, such as light-coloured vegetables and meats. It can also be used in preparing **sumashijiru** (clear soup) and one-pot meals such as **yosenabe**.

Shungiku (chrysanthemum leaves)

These edible leaves are very high in Vitamin A, are used in many one-pots and other dishes. The plant should not be confused with the ordinary Western garden varieties of chrysanthemum, which are not edible.

Soba noodles (buckwheat noodles)

Sold dry in 500g packages, they are greyish-brown in colour.

Somen noodles (fine wheat noodles)

Su (vinegar)

This sour seasoning contains 3 to 5 per cent acetic acid. There are brewed and synthetic types, but the synthetic ones are less mild and sweet than the brewed ones and are more sour. Among the brewed types, most often used in cooking, those made from rice *yone-su* and *sake* less *kasu-zu* are the most common. Vinegar is an essential ingredient in making *sushi*, vinegared dishes *sunomono* and in pickling. It is employed in a wide range of other uses to prevent discolouration of peeled vegetables, such as burdock root and lotus root, and to soften bones in small fish when boiled. Cider vinegar is probably the best substitute.

Sudare

A bamboo mat made of thin slats of bamboo very like a bamboo placemat, which may be used as a substitute, used for rolling omelettes, *sushi* and vegetables such as spinach.

Sukiyaki-Nabe

A round, cast-iron pan used for cooking *sukiyaki*. A cast-iron frying-pan is a good substitute.

Sukiyaki Sauce

A soy sauce-based seasoning with sugar and rice wine added, this sauce is very convenient for *sukiyaki* cooking.

Sunomono

Foods in a vinegared dressing such as salads. This category overlaps with **aemono**, dressed salads. Both types of dish are served as accompaniments to main courses.

Suribachi

A serrated earthernware bowl used with a **surikogi**, a wooden pestle. Makes grinding nuts and other foods easy. Use chopsticks to scrape down the sides. A small coffee mill or nut grinder is a substitute.

Sushi

Vinegared rich dishes usually topped with raw fish.

Sushioke

Also called a **bandai**, is a round, shallow wooden dish for **sushi**.

T

Tai (sea bream)

In Japan, it is the most valued fish. It can be used diversely, such as for **sashimi**, in stock-based dishes, or can be grilled.

Takenoki (bamboo shoots)

Tinned whole shoots are available in Chinese and Japanese shops and sometimes in groceries and supermarkets.

Tamari

Used in oriental cooking and sold in health food stores, this is a thick, very dark liquid with a stronger flavour than soy sauce and a clear fine soy aroma. It is sometimes described as unfermented or raw soy because of its shorter brewing period.

Teriyaki
The technique of glazing food in a soy sauce and **mirin** mixture either in a frying-pan or under a grill.

Takegushi
Small bamboo skewers resembling large toothpicks.

Tamago-Yaki Nabe
A rectangular frying-pan used specially for making rolled omelettes. Though any frying-pan may be used, the oblong shape makes rolled omelettes easier and gives them a neater look.

Tempura Pan
A round iron pan for deep frying with a built-in draining rack on one side. Ideal for all **agemono** (deep-fried dishes). A deep-fat fryer, or a heavy iron frying-pan may be used instead.

Tofu (bean curd)
The milky-white, custard-like bean-curd cake is a Chinese invention. Soya beans are boiled and crushed, then a coagulant is added to form the curds. If the curds are then drained, the result is 'cotton' **tofu**, the standard type; if they are not, a more delicate and fragile **tofu** (called 'silk') is produced.

Cotton **tofu**, the most readily available, will do for most recipes. Fresh **tofu** is sold in water-filled plastic tubs, date-stamped to indicate freshness, in health food shops. Store **tofu** in plenty of cold water, under refrigeration; change the water every day.

Togarashi (whole dried hot red chilies)
When ground and put in containers the peppers are called **togarashi-ko** and are used as an on-the-table condiment. Any dried hot red chili may be used. For ground pepper, cayenne is a good substitute.

Tori-Sasami
Bamboo-leaf chicken breasts. These are the two smaller fillets of the skinned and boned whole chicken breast and in Japan are considered the best part. Save the two larger fillets for another use.

Tororo Konbu (shredded kelp seaweed)

Toso
Cold spiced **mirin**, a traditional New Year drink.

Tsukemono

Pickled vegetables available bottled or in vacuum-sealed plastic bags.

U

Udon (white noodles)

Made of wheat flour, these noodles are available in several thicknesses and lengths. Dried **udon** are packaged in 100g individual portions, each of which provides about four or five servings.

Umeboshi (pickled plums)

These are soaked in brine, packed in **shiso** leaves and left to mature in a salty mix. They have long been respected as an aid to digestion and keeping the intestinal tract clear. Purchased in bottled form, once opened and refrigerated they can be kept indefinitely.

Uni (sea urchins)

Available as prepared paste in jars. Will keep indefinitely, refrigerated.

Usukuchi Shoyu

Light soy sauce.

Uzura Tamago (quail eggs)

Ready cooked and available in tins.

W

Wakame (seaweed)

Bought in dried form it must be softened in tepid water for 20 minutes before use.

Wakame is widely used in soups. It is highly nutritious and low in kilojoules as well as being decorative in colour and shape.

Wakegi (scallions)

These onions are thinner and softer and not as strong as negi.

Warabi (bracken)

A fern used in one-pot cooking, steamed dishes and pickles; bracken can be bought dried or vacuum packed from Asian food stores.

Wasabi (Japanese horseradish)

This green root is hot and has a strong aroma. It is sold as a seasoning in raw, powdered or paste form ready for use. When used raw, it is grated. The powdered form is dissolved in water and made into a paste. It is used sparingly with **sashimi** and hand-formed **nigiri-zushi**, and dressed dishes **aemono**.

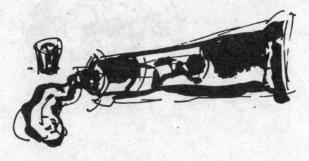

Y

Yakidofu

Grilled soy bean curd.

Yama-Gobou

A root vegetable in between a radish and a carrot in taste. **Yama-gobou** can be bought in packets.

Yuba

Dried soy bean curd packaged in rolls or in flat sheets.

Yuzu (citron)

The *yuzu* fragrance is unique and resembles no citrus fruit of the west. The yellow fruit, about the size of a tangerine, has a very short season. Lime or lemon can be substituted for *yuzu*.

Z

Zaru

Plate-like bamboo strainers used for straining foods, especially noodles for summer dishes. They may also be used as serving plates.

Zukemono

Pickled vegetables available in bottled and vacuum packs.